Getting Started with Julia Programming

Enter the exciting world of Julia, a high-performance language for technical computing

Ivo Balbaert

[PACKT] **PUBLISHING**

BIRMINGHAM - MUMBAI

Getting Started with Julia Programming

First published: February 2015

Production reference: 1200215

Published by Packt Publishing Ltd.
Livery Place
35 Livery Street
Birmingham B3 2PB, UK.

ISBN 978-1-78328-479-5

www.packtpub.com

Credits

Author
Ivo Balbaert

Reviewers
Pascal Bugnion
Michael Otte
Dustin E. Stansbury

Commissioning Editor
Kevin Colaco

Acquisition Editor
Kevin Colaco

Content Development Editor
Neeshma Ramakrishnan

Technical Editors
Mrunmayee Patil
Shali Sasidharan

Copy Editor
Rashmi Sawant

Project Coordinator
Purav Motiwalla

Proofreaders
Mario Cecere
Paul Hindle

Indexer
Monica Ajmera Mehta

Production Coordinator
Conidon Miranda

Cover Work
Conidon Miranda

About the Author

Ivo Balbaert is currently a lecturer in (web) programming and databases at CVO Antwerpen (www.cvoantwerpen.be), a community college in Belgium. He received a PhD degree in applied physics from the University of Antwerp in 1986. He worked for 20 years in the software industry as a developer and consultant in several companies, and for 10 years as a project manager at the University Hospital of Antwerp. From 2000 onward, he switched to partly teaching and developing software (KHM Mechelen, CVO Antwerp).

He also wrote an introductory book in Dutch about developing in Ruby and Rails, *Programmeren met Ruby en Rails*, *Van Duuren Media*. In 2012, he authored a book on the Go programming language, *The Way To Go*, *iUniverse*. In 2013, in collaboration with Dzenan Ridzanovic, he authored *Learning Dart* and *Dart Cookbook*, both by Packt Publishing.

I would like to thank the technical reviewers Pascal Bugnion, Michael Otte, and Dustin Stansbury for the many useful remarks that improved the text.

About the Reviewers

Pascal Bugnion is a data scientist with a strong analytical background as well as a passion for software development. He pursued a materials science undergraduate degree at Oxford University. He then went on to complete a PhD in computational physics at Cambridge University, during which he developed and applied the quantum Monte Carlo methods to solidstate physics. This resulted in four publications, including an article in *Physical Review Letters*, the leading physics journal. He now works as a database architect for SCL Elections, a company that specializes in predicting voter behavior.

Pascal is strongly interested in contributing to open source software, especially the Python scientific stack. He has contributed to NumPy, matplotlib, and IPython, and maintains ScikitMonaco, a Python library for Monte Carlo integration as well as GMaps, a Python module for embedding Google maps in IPython notebooks.

Michael Otte has interests that include the application of artificial intelligence to robotics, with a focus on path planning algorithms and multirobot systems. He has been using the Julia language since 2012 to implement motion planning, graph search, and other algorithms, many of which have appeared in top peer-reviewed publications. See www.ottelab.com for more details. He is currently a research associate with the Department of Aerospace Engineering Sciences at the University of Colorado at Boulder. Prior to this, he was a postdoctoral associate with the Laboratory for Information and Decision Systems (LIDS) at the Massachusetts Institute of Technology. He received his PhD and MS degrees at the University of Colorado at Boulder in computer science and a BS degree in aeronautical engineering and computer science from Clarkson University.

Dustin Stansbury received his BS degree in both physics and psychology from Appalachian State University and his PhD degree in vision science from the University of California, Berkeley. His graduate research focused on developing hierarchical statistical models of the mammalian visual and auditory systems. He currently works in the field of music retrieval and regularly contributes to his machine learning blog, `theclevermachine`.

Dustin has contributed a chapter to the text book, *Scene Vision: Making sense of what we see*, MIT Press 2014, Cambridge MA.

www.PacktPub.com

Support files, eBooks, discount offers, and more

For support files and downloads related to your book, please visit www.PacktPub.com.

Did you know that Packt offers eBook versions of every book published, with PDF and ePub files available? You can upgrade to the eBook version at www.PacktPub.com and as a print book customer, you are entitled to a discount on the eBook copy. Get in touch with us at service@packtpub.com for more details.

At www.PacktPub.com, you can also read a collection of free technical articles, sign up for a range of free newsletters and receive exclusive discounts and offers on Packt books and eBooks.

https://www2.packtpub.com/books/subscription/packtlib

Do you need instant solutions to your IT questions? PacktLib is Packt's online digital book library. Here, you can search, access, and read Packt's entire library of books.

Why subscribe?
- Fully searchable across every book published by Packt
- Copy and paste, print, and bookmark content
- On demand and accessible via a web browser

Free access for Packt account holders

If you have an account with Packt at www.PacktPub.com, you can use this to access PacktLib today and view 9 entirely free books. Simply use your login credentials for immediate access.

Table of Contents

Preface

Julia is a new programming language that was developed at MIT in the Applied Computing Group under the supervision of Prof. Alan Edelman. Its development started in 2009, and it was first presented publicly in February 2012. It is still a fairly young language when you look at the current Version number (0.3), but its foundation is stable; the core language has had no backwards incompatible changes since Version 0.1. It is based on clear and solid principles, and its popularity is steadily increasing in the technical, data scientist, and high-performance computing arenas. In the section *The Rationale for Julia*, we present an overview of the principles on which Julia is based and compare them to other languages.

What this book covers

Chapter 1, *Installing the Julia Platform*, guides you with the installation of all the necessary components required for a Julia environment. It teaches you how to work with Julia's console (the REPL) and discusses some of the more elaborate development editors you can use.

Chapter 2, *Variables, Types, and Operations*, discusses the elementary built-in types in Julia, and the operations that can be performed on them, so that you are prepared to start writing the code with them.

Chapter 3, *Functions*, explains why functions are the basic building blocks of Julia, and how to effectively use them.

Chapter 4, *Control Flow*, shows Julia's elegant control constructs, how to perform error handling, and how to use coroutines (called Tasks in Julia) to structure the execution of your code.

Chapter 5, *Collection Types*, explores the different types that group individual values, such as arrays and matrices, tuples, dictionaries, and sets.

Chapter 6, More on Types, Methods, and Modules, digs deeper into the type concept and explains how this is used in multiple dispatch to get C-like performance. Modules, a higher code organizing concept, are discussed as well.

Chapter 7, Metaprogramming in Julia, touches on the deeper layers of Julia, such as expressions and reflection capabilities, and demonstrates the power of macros.

Chapter 8, I/O, Networking, and Parallel Computing, shows how to work with data in files and databases using DataFrames. We can explore the networking capabilities, and shows how to set up a parallel computing environment with Julia.

Chapter 9, Running External Programs, looks at how Julia interacts with the command line and other languages and also discusses performance tips.

Chapter 10, The Standard Library and Packages, digs deeper into the standard library and demonstrates the important packages for visualization of data.

Appendix, List of Macros and Packages, provides you with handy reference lists of the macros and packages used in this book.

What you need for this book

To run the code examples in the book, you will need the Julia platform for your computer, which can be downloaded from http://julialang.org/downloads/. To work more comfortably with Julia scripts, a development environment such as IJulia, Sublime Text, or LightTable is advisable. *Chapter 1, Installing the Julia Platform*, contains detailed instructions to set up your Julia environment.

Who this book is for

This book is intended for the data scientist and for all those who work in technical and scientific computation projects. It will get you up and running quickly with Julia to start simplifying your projects applications. The book assumes that you already have some basic working knowledge of high-level dynamic languages such as MATLAB, R, Python, or Ruby.

Conventions

In this book, you will find a number of text styles that distinguish between different kinds of information. Here are some examples of these styles and an explanation of their meaning.

Code words in text, database table names, folder names, filenames, file extensions, pathnames, dummy URLs, user input, and Twitter handles are shown as follows: "As an example, we use the data-file `winequality.csv` that contains 1599 sample measurements, 12 data columns."

A block of code is set as follows:

```
using DataFrames
fname = "winequality.csv"
data = readtable(fname, separator = ';')
```

When we wish to draw your attention to a particular part of a code block, the relevant lines or items are set in bold:

```
using DataFrames
fname = "winequality.csv"
data = readtable(fname, separator = ';')
```

Any command-line input or output is written as follows:

```
julia main.jl
```

New terms and **important words** are shown in bold. Words that you see on the screen, for example, in menus or dialog boxes, appear in the text like this: "Navigate to **Configuration | System Administration | ODBC Data Sources**."

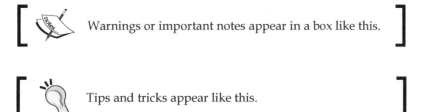

Warnings or important notes appear in a box like this.

Tips and tricks appear like this.

Reader feedback

Feedback from our readers is always welcome. Let us know what you think about this book—what you liked or disliked. Reader feedback is important for us as it helps us develop titles that you will really get the most out of.

To send us general feedback, simply e-mail feedback@packtpub.com, and mention the book's title in the subject of your message.

If there is a topic that you have expertise in and you are interested in either writing or contributing to a book, see our author guide at www.packtpub.com/authors.

Customer support

Now that you are the proud owner of a Packt book, we have a number of things to help you to get the most from your purchase.

Downloading the example code

You can download the example code files from your account at http://www.packtpub.com for all the Packt Publishing books you have purchased. If you purchased this book elsewhere, you can visit http://www.packtpub.com/support and register to have the files e-mailed directly to you.

Errata

Although we have taken every care to ensure the accuracy of our content, mistakes do happen. If you find a mistake in one of our books—maybe a mistake in the text or the code—we would be grateful if you could report this to us. By doing so, you can save other readers from frustration and help us improve subsequent versions of this book. If you find any errata, please report them by visiting http://www.packtpub.com/submit-errata, selecting your book, clicking on the **Errata Submission Form** link, and entering the details of your errata. Once your errata are verified, your submission will be accepted and the errata will be uploaded to our website or added to any list of existing errata under the Errata section of that title.

To view the previously submitted errata, go to https://www.packtpub.com/books/content/support and enter the name of the book in the search field. The required information will appear under the **Errata** section.

Piracy

Piracy of copyrighted material on the Internet is an ongoing problem across all media. At Packt, we take the protection of our copyright and licenses very seriously. If you come across any illegal copies of our works in any form on the Internet, please provide us with the location address or website name immediately so that we can pursue a remedy.

Please contact us at copyright@packtpub.com with a link to the suspected pirated material.

We appreciate your help in protecting our authors and our ability to bring you valuable content.

Questions

If you have a problem with any aspect of this book, you can contact us at questions@packtpub.com, and we will do our best to address the problem.

The Rationale for Julia

This introduction will present you with the reasons why Julia is quickly growing in popularity in the technical, data scientist, and high-performance computing arena. We will cover the following topics:

- The scope of Julia
- Julia's place among other programming languages
- A comparison with other languages for the data scientist
- Useful links

The scope of Julia

The core designers and developers of Julia (*Jeff Bezanson*, *Stefan Karpinski*, and *Viral Shah*) have made it clear that Julia was born out of a deep frustration with the existing software toolset in the technical computing disciplines. Basically, it boils down to the following dilemma:

- Prototyping is a problem in this domain that needs a high-level, easy-to-use, and flexible language that lets the developer concentrate on the problem itself instead of on low-level details of the language and computation.

- The actual computation of a problem needs maximum performance; a factor of 10 in computation time makes a world of difference (think of one day versus ten days), so the production version often has to be (re)written in C or FORTRAN.

- Before Julia, practitioners had to be satisfied with a *"speed for convenience"* trade-off, use developer-friendly and expressive, but decades-old interpreted languages such as MATLAB, R, or Python to express the problem at a high level. To program the performance-sensitive parts and speed up the actual computation, people had to resort to statically compiled languages such as C or FORTRAN, or even the assembly code. Mastery on both the levels is not evident: writing high-level code in MATLAB, R, or Python for prototyping on the one hand, and writing code that does the same thing in C, which is used for the actual execution.

  Julia was explicitly designed to bridge this gap. It gives you the possibility of writing high-performance code that uses CPU and memory resources as effectively as can be done in C, but working in pure Julia all the way down, reduces the need for a low-level language. This way, you can rapidly iterate using a simple programming model from the problem prototype to near-C performance. The Julia developers have proven that working in one environment that has the expressive capabilities as well as the pure speed is possible using the recent advances in **Low Level Virtual Machine Just in Time (LLVM JIT)** compiler technologies (for more information, see `http://en.wikipedia.org/wiki/LLVM`).

In summary, they designed Julia to have the following specifications:

- Julia is open source and free with a liberal (MIT) license.

- It is designed to be an easy-to-use and learn, elegant, clear and dynamic, interactive language by reducing the development time. To that end, Julia almost looks like the pseudo code with an obvious and familiar mathematical notation; for example, here is the definition for a polynomial function, straight from the code:

  ```
  x -> 7x^3 + 30x^2 + 5x + 42
  ```

  Notice that there is no need to indicate the multiplications.

- It provides the computational power and speed without having to leave the Julia environment.

- Metaprogramming and macro capabilities (due to its homoiconicity (refer to *Chapter 7*, *Metaprogramming in Julia*), inherited from Lisp), to increase its abstraction power.

- Also, it is usable for general programming purposes, not only in pure computing disciplines.

- It has built-in and simple to use concurrent and parallel capabilities to thrive in the multicore world of today and tomorrow.

Julia unites this all in one environment, something which was thought impossible until now by most researchers and language designers.

The Julia logo

Julia's place among the other programming languages

Julia reconciles and brings together the technologies that before were considered separate, namely:

- The dynamic, untyped, and interpreted languages on the one hand (Python, Ruby, Perl, MATLAB/Octave, R, and so on)
- The statically typed and compiled languages on the other (C, C++, Fortran, and Fortress)

How can Julia have the flexibility of the first and the speed of the second category?

Julia has no static compilation step. The machine code is generated just-in-time by an LLVM-based JIT compiler. This compiler, together with the design of the language, helps Julia to achieve maximal performance for numerical, technical, and scientific computing. The key for the performance is the *type information*, which is gathered by a fully automatic and intelligent *type inference engine*, that deduces the type from the data contained in the variables. Indeed, because Julia has a *dynamic type system*, declaring the type of variables in the code is optional. Indicating types is not necessary, but it can be done to document the code, improve tooling possibilities, or in some cases, to give hints to the compiler to choose a more optimized execution path. This optional typing discipline is an aspect it shares with Dart. Typeless Julia is a valid and useful subset of the language, similar to traditional dynamic languages, but it nevertheless runs at statically compiled speeds. Julia applies *generic programming* and *polymorphic functions* to the limit, writing an algorithm just once and applying it to a broad range of types. This provides common functionality across drastically different types, for example: `size` is a generic function with 50 concrete method implementations. A system called **dynamic multiple dispatch** efficiently picks the optimal method for all of a function's arguments from tens of method definitions. Depending on the actual types very specific and efficient native code implementations of the function are chosen or generated, so its type system lets it align closer with primitive machine operations.

In summary, data flow-based type inference implies multiple dispatch choosing specialized execution code.

However, do keep in mind that types are not statically checked. Exceptions due to type errors can occur at runtime, so thorough testing is mandatory. As to categorizing Julia in the programming language universe, it embodies multiple paradigms, such as procedural, functional, metaprogramming, and also (but not fully) object oriented. It is by no means an exclusively class-based language such as Java, Ruby, or C#. Nevertheless, its *type system* offers a kind of inheritance and is very powerful. Conversions and promotions for numeric and other types are elegant, friendly, and swift, and user-defined types are as fast and compact as built-in types. As for functional programming, Julia makes it very easy to design programs with pure functions and has no side effects; functions are first-class objects, as in mathematics.

Julia also supports a multiprocessing environment based on a message passing model to allow programs to run via multiple processes (local or remote) using distributed arrays, enabling distributed programs based on any of the models for parallel programming.

Julia is equally suited for general programming as is Python. It has as good and modern (Unicode capable) string processing and regular expressions as Perl or other languages. Moreover, it can also be used at the shell level, as a glue language to synchronize the execution of other programs or to manage other processes.

Julia has a standard library written in Julia itself, and a built-in package manager based on GitHub, which is called **Metadata**, to work with a steadily growing collection of external libraries called **packages**. It is *cross platform*, supporting GNU/Linux, Darwin/OS X, Windows, and FreeBSD for both x86/64 (64-bit) and x86 (32-bit) architectures.

A comparison with other languages for the data scientist

Because speed is one of the ultimate targets of Julia, a benchmark comparison with other languages is displayed prominently on the Julia website (`http://julialang.org/`). It shows that Julia's rivals C and Fortran, often stay within a factor of two of fully optimized C code, and leave the traditional dynamic language category far behind. One of Julia's explicit goals is to have sufficiently good performance that you never have to drop down into C. This is in contrast to the following environments, where (even for NumPy) you often have to work with C to get enough performance when moving to production. So, a new era of technical computing can be envisioned, where libraries can be developed in a high-level language instead of in C or FORTRAN. Julia is especially good at running MATLAB and R-style programs. Let's compare them somewhat more in detail.

MATLAB

Julia is instantly familiar to MATLAB users; its syntax strongly resembles that of MATLAB, but Julia aims to be a much more general purpose language than MATLAB. The names of most functions in Julia correspond to the MATLAB/Octave names, and not the R names. Under the covers, however, the way the computations are done, things are extremely different. Julia also has equally powerful capabilities in *linear algebra*, the field where MATLAB is traditionally applied. However, using Julia won't give you the same license fee headaches. Moreover, the benchmarks show that it is from 10 to 1,000 times faster depending on the type of operation, also when compared to Octave (the open source version of MATLAB). Julia provides an interface to the MATLAB language with the package `MATLAB.jl` (`https://github.com/lindahua/MATLAB.jl`).

R

R was until now the chosen development language in the *statistics* domain. Julia proves to be as usable as R in this domain, but again with a performance increase of a factor of 10 to 1,000. Doing statistics in MATLAB is frustrating, as is doing linear algebra in R, but Julia fits both the purposes. Julia has a much richer type system than the vector-based types of R. Some statistics experts such as *Douglas Bates* heavily support and promote Julia as well. Julia provides an interface to the R language with the package `Rif.jl` (`https://github.com/lgautier/Rif.jl`).

Python

Again, Julia has a performance head start of a factor of 10 to 30 times as compared to Python. However, Julia compiles the code that reads like Python into machine code that performs like C. Furthermore, if necessary you can call Python functions from within Julia using the `PyCall` package (`https://github.com/stevengj/PyCall.jl`).

Because of the huge number of existing libraries in all these languages, any practical data scientist can and will need to mix the Julia code with R or Python when the problem at hand demands it.

Julia can also be applied to *data analysis and big data*, because these often involve predictive analysis, modeling problems that can often be reduced to linear algebra algorithms, or graph analysis techniques, all things Julia is good at tackling.

In the field of **High Performance Computing (HPC)**, a language such as Julia has long been lacking. With Julia, domain experts can experiment and quickly and easily express a problem in such a way that they can use modern HPC hardware as easily as a desktop PC. In other words, a language that gets users started quickly without the need to understand the details of the underlying machine architecture is very welcome in this area.

Useful links

The following are the links that can be useful while using Julia:

- The main Julia website can be found at http://julialang.org/

- For documentation, refer to http://docs.julialang.org/en/latest

- View the packages at http://pkg.julialang.org/indexorg.html

- Subscribe to the mailing lists at http://julialang.org/community/

- Get support at an IRC channel from http://webchat.freenode.net/?channels=julia

Summary

In this introduction, we gave an overview of Julia's characteristics and compared them to the existing languages in its field. Julia's main advantage is its ability to generate specialized code for different input types. When coupled with the compiler's ability to infer these types, this makes it possible to write the Julia code at an abstract level while achieving the efficiency associated with the low-level code. Julia is already quite stable and production ready. The learning curve for Julia is very gentle; the idea being that people who don't care about fancy language features should be able to use it productively too and learn about new features only when they become useful or needed.

Installing the Julia Platform

1

This chapter guides you through the download and installation of all the necessary components of Julia. The topics covered in this chapter are as follows:

- Installing Julia
- Working with Julia's shell
- Start-up options and Julia scripts
- Packages
- Installing and working with Julia Studio
- Installing and working with IJulia
- Installing Sublime-IJulia
- Installing Juno
- Other editors and IDEs
- Working of Julia

By the end of this chapter, you will have a running Julia platform. Moreover, you will be able to work with Julia's shell as well as with editors or integrated development environments with a lot of built-in features to make development more comfortable.

Installing Julia

The Julia platform in binary (that is, executable) form can be downloaded from http://julialang.org/downloads/. It exists for three major platforms (Windows, Linux, and OS X) in 32- and 64-bit format, and is delivered as a package or in an archive format. You should use the current official stable release when doing serious professional work with Julia (at the time of writing, this is Version 0.3). If you would like to investigate the latest developments, install the upcoming version (which is now Version 0.4). The previous link contains detailed and platform-specific instructions for the installation. We will not repeat these instructions here completely, but we will summarize some important points.

Windows version – usable from Windows XP SP2 onwards

You need to keep the following things in mind if you are using the Windows OS:

1. As a prerequisite, you need the 7zip extractor program, so first download and install http://www.7-zip.org/download.html.

2. Now, download the julia-n.m.p-win64.exe file to a temporary folder (n.m.p is the version number, such as 0.2.1 or 0.3.0; win32/win64 are respectively the 32- and 64-bit version; a release candidate file looks like julia-0.4.0-rc1-nnnnnnn-win64 (nnnnnnn is a checksum number such as 0480f1b).

3. Double-click on the file (or right-click, and select **Run as Administrator** if you want Julia installed for all users on the machine). Clicking **OK** on the security dialog message, and then choosing the installation directory (for example, c:\julia) will extract the archive into the chosen folder, producing the following directory structure, and taking some 400 MB of disk space:

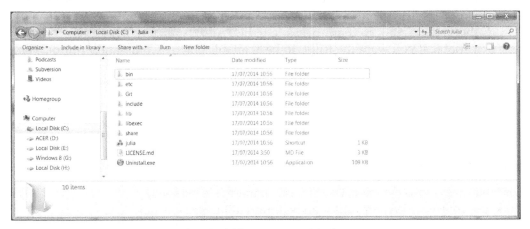

The Julia folder structure in Windows

4. A menu shortcut will be created which, when clicked, starts the Julia command-line version or **Read Evaluate Print Loop** (REPL), as shown in the following screenshot:

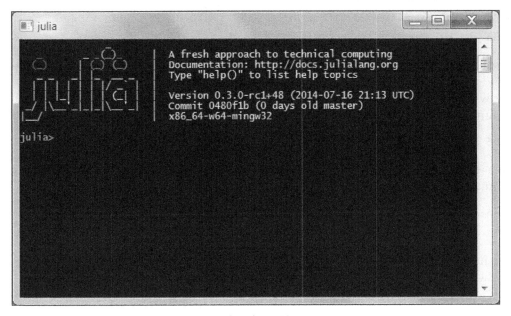

The Julia REPL

5. On Windows, if you have chosen C:\Julia as your installation directory, this is the C:\Julia\bin\julia.exe file. Add C:\Julia\bin to your PATH variable if you want the REPL to be available on any Command Prompt. The default installation folder on Windows is: C:\Users\UserName\AppData\Local\Julia-n.m.p (where n.m.p is the version number, such as 0.3.2).

6. More information on Julia in the Windows OS can be found at https://github.com/JuliaLang/julia/blob/master/README.windows.md.

Ubuntu version

For Ubuntu systems (Version 12.04 or later), there is a **Personal Package Archive** (**PPA**) for Julia (can be found at https://launchpad.net/~staticfloat/+archive/ubuntu/juliareleases) that makes the installation painless. All you need to do to get the stable version is to issue the following commands in a terminal session:

```
sudo add-apt-repository ppa:staticfloat/juliareleases
sudo add-apt-repository ppa:staticfloat/julia-deps
sudo apt-get update
sudo apt-get install julia
```

If you want to be at the bleeding edge of development, you can download the nightly builds instead of the stable releases. The nightly builds are generally less stable, but will contain the most recent features. To do so, replace the first of the preceding commands with:

```
sudo add-apt-repository ppa:staticfloat/julianightlies
```

This way, you can always upgrade to a more recent version by issuing the following commands:

```
sudo apt-get update
sudo apt-get upgrade
```

The Julia executable lives in /usr/bin/julia (given by the JULIA_HOME variable or by the which julia command) and the standard library is installed in /usr/share/julia/base, with shared libraries in /usr/lib/x86_64-linux-gnu/Julia.

For other Linux versions, the best way to get Julia running is to build from source (refer to the next section).

OS X

Installation for OS X is straightforward—using the standard software installation tools for the platform. Add `/Applications/Julia-n.m.app/Contents/Resources/julia/bin/Julia` to make Julia available everywhere on your computer.

If you want code to be run whenever you start a Julia session, put it in `/home/.juliarc.jl` on Ubuntu, `~/.juliarc.jl` on OS X, or `c:\Users\username\.juliarc.jl` on Windows. For instance, if this file contains the following code:

```
println("Greetings! 你好! 안녕하세요?")
```

Then, Julia starts up in its shell (or REPL as it is usually called) with the following text in the screenshot, which shows its character representation capabilities:

Using .juliarc.jl

Building from source

Perform the following steps to build Julia from source:

1. Download the source code, rather than the binaries, if you intend to contribute to the development of Julia itself, or if no Julia binaries are provided for your operating system or particular computer architecture. Building from source is quite straightforward on Ubuntu, so we will outline the procedure here. The Julia source code can be found on GitHub at `https://github.com/JuliaLang/julia.git`.

2. Compiling these will get you the latest Julia version, not the stable version (if you want the latter, download the binaries, and refer to the previous section).

3. Make sure you have git installed; if not, issue the command:

   ```
   sudo apt-get -f install git
   ```

4. Then, clone the Julia sources with the following command:

   ```
   git clone git://github.com/JuliaLang/julia.git
   ```

   This will download the Julia source code into a julia directory in the current folder.

5. The Julia building process needs the GNU compilation tools g++, gfortran, and m4, so make sure that you have installed them with the following command:

   ```
   sudo apt-get install gfortran g++ m4
   ```

6. Now go to the Julia folder and start the compilation process as follows:

   ```
   cd julia
   make
   ```

7. After a successful build, Julia starts up with the ./julia command.

8. Afterwards, if you want to download and compile the newest version, here are the commands to do this in the Julia source directory:

   ```
   git pull
   make clean
   make
   ```

For more information on how to build Julia on Windows, OS X, and other systems, refer to https://github.com/JuliaLang/julia/.

> **Using parallelization**
>
> If you want Julia to use *n* concurrent processes, compile the source with make -j n.

There are two ways of using Julia. As described in the previous section, we can use the Julia shell for interactive work. Alternatively, we can write programs in a text file, save them with a .jl extension, and let Julia execute the whole program sequentially.

Working with Julia's shell

We started with Julia's shell in the previous section (refer to the preceding two screenshots) to verify the correctness of the installation, by issuing the `julia` command in a terminal session. The shell or REPL is Julia's working environment, where you can interact with the **Just in Time (JIT)** compiler to test out pieces of code. When satisfied, you can copy and paste this code into a file with a `.jl` extension, such as `program.jl`. Alternatively, you can continue the work on this code from within a text editor or an IDE, such as the ones we will point out later in this chapter. After the banner with Julia's logo has appeared, you get a `julia>` prompt for the input. To end this session, and get to the OS Command Prompt, type *CTRL + D* or `quit()`, and hit *ENTER*. To evaluate an expression, type it and press *ENTER* to show the result, as shown in the following screenshot:

Working with the REPL (1)

If, for some reason, you don't need to see the result, end the expression with a `;` (semicolon) such as `6 * 7`. In both the cases, the resulting value is stored, for convenience, in a variable named `ans` that can be used in expressions, but only inside the REPL. You can bind a value to a variable by entering an assignment as `a = 3`. Julia is dynamic, and we don't need to enter a type for `a`, but we do need to enter a value for the variable, so that Julia can infer its type. Using a variable `b` that is not bound to the `a` value, results in the `ERROR: b not defined` message. Strings are delineated by double quotes (`""`), as in `b = "Julia"`. The following screenshot illustrates these workings with the REPL:

Working with the REPL (2)

Previous expressions can be retrieved in the same session by working with the up and down arrow keys. The following key bindings are also handy:

- To clear or interrupt a current command, press *CTRL + C*
- To clear the screen (but variables are kept in memory), press *CTRL + L*
- To reset the session so that variables are cleared, enter the command `workspace()` in the REPL

Commands from the previous sessions can still be retrieved, because they are stored (with a timestamp) in a `.julia_history` file (in /home/$USER on Ubuntu, c:\Users\ username on Windows, or ~/.julia_history on OS X). *Ctrl + R* (produces a (reverse-i-search) ': prompt) searches through these commands.

Typing *?* starts up the help mode (`help?>`) to give quick access to Julia's documentation. Information on function names, types, macros, and so on, is given when typing in their name. Alternatively, to get more information on a variable a, type `help(a)`, and to get more information on a function such as `sort`, type `help(sort)`. To find all the places where a function such as `println` is defined or used, type `apropos("println")`, which gives the following output:

```
Base.println(x)
```

```
Base.enumerate(iter)
```

```
Base.cartesianmap(f, dims)
```

Thus, we can see that it is defined in the `Base` module, and is used in two other functions. Different complete expressions on the same line have to be separated by a `;` (semicolon) and only the last result is shown. You can enter multi-line expressions as shown in the following screenshot. If the shell detects that the statement is syntactically incomplete, it will not attempt to evaluate it. Rather, it will wait for the user to enter additional lines until the multi-line statement can be evaluated.

Working with the REPL (3)

A handy autocomplete feature also exists. Type one or more letters, press the *Tab* key twice, and then a list of functions starting with these letters appears. For example: type so, press the *Tab* key twice, and then you get the list as: sort sort! sortby sortby! sortcols sortperm sortrows.

If you start a line with ;, the rest of the line is interpreted as a system shell command (try for example, ls, cd, mkdir, whoami, and so on). The *Backspace* key returns to the Julia prompt.

A Julia script can be executed in the REPL by calling it with include. For example, for hello.jl, which contains the println("Hello, Julia World!") command, the command is as follows:

```
julia> include("hello.jl")
```

The preceding command prints the output as follows:

```
Hello, Julia World!
```

Experiment a bit with different expressions to get some feeling for this environment.

You can get more information at http://docs.julialang.org/en/ latest/manual/interacting-with-julia/#key-bindings.

Startup options and Julia scripts

Without any options, the julia command starts up the REPL environment. A useful option to check your environment is julia -v. This shows Julia's version, for example, julia-version 0.3.2+2. (The versioninfo() function in REPL is more detailed, the VERSION constant gives you only the version number: v"0.3.2+2"). An option that lets you evaluate expressions on the command line itself is -e, for example:

```
julia -e 'a = 6 * 7;
println(a)'
```

The preceding commands print out 42 (on Windows, use " instead of the ' character).

Some other options useful for parallel processing will be discussed in *Chapter 9, Running External Programs*. Type julia -h for a list of all options.

A `script.jl` file with Julia source code can be started from the command line with the following command:

```
julia script.jl arg1 arg2 arg3
```

Here `arg1`, `arg2`, and `arg3` are optional arguments to be used in the script's code. They are available from the global constant `ARGS`. Take a look at the `args.jl` file as follows:

```
for arg in ARGS
  println(arg)
end
```

The `julia args.jl 1 Dart C` command prints out `1`, `Dart`, and `C` on consecutive lines.

A script file also can execute other source files by including them in the REPL; for example, `main.jl` contains `include("hello.jl")` that will execute the code from `hello.jl` when called with `julia main.jl`.

Downloading the example code

You can download the example code files from your account at `http://www.packtpub.com` for all the Packt Publishing books you have purchased. If you purchased this book elsewhere, you can visit `http://www.packtpub.com/support` and register to have the files e-mailed directly to you.

Packages

Most of the standard library in Julia (can be found in `/share/julia/base` relative to where Julia was installed) is written in Julia itself. The rest of Julia's code ecosystem is contained in packages that are simply `Git` repositories. They are most often authored by external contributors, and already provide functionality for such diverse disciplines such as bioinformatics, chemistry, cosmology, finance, linguistics, machine learning, mathematics, statistics, and high-performance computing. A searchable package list can be found at `http://pkg.julialang.org/`. Official Julia packages are registered in the `METADATA.jl` file in the Julia Git repository, available on GitHub at `https://github.com/JuliaLang/METADATA.jl`.

Julia's installation contains a built-in package manager `Pkg` for installing additional Julia packages written in Julia. The downloaded packages are stored in a cache ready to be used by Julia given by `Pkg.dir()`, which are located at `c:\users\username\.julia\vn.m\.cache`, `/home/$USER/.julia/vn.m/.cache`, or `~/.julia/vn.m/.cache`. If you want to check which packages are installed, run the `Pkg.status()` command in the Julia REPL, to get a list of packages with their versions, as shown in the following screenshot:

```
julia> Pkg.status()
4 required packages:
 - IJulia                      0.1.12
 - Jewel                       0.6.2
 - Nettle                      0.1.4
 - ZMQ                         0.1.12
11 additional packages:
 - BinDeps                     0.2.14
 - HTTPClient                  0.1.4
 - JSON                        0.3.7
 - Lazy                        0.4.1
 - LibCURL                     0.1.3
 - LibExpat                    0.0.4
 - REPLCompletions             0.0.1
 - URIParser                   0.0.2
 - URLParse                    0.0.0
 - WinRPM                      0.0.14
 - Zlib                        0.1.7
```

Packages list

The `Pkg.installed()` command gives you the same information, but in a dictionary form and is usable in code. Version and dependency management is handled automatically by `Pkg`. Different versions of Julia can coexist with incompatible packages, each version has its own package cache.

If you get an error with `Pkg.status()` such as `ErrorException("Unable to read directory METADATA.")`, issue a `Pkg.init()` command to create the package repository folders, and clone METADATA from Git. If the problem is not easy to find or the cache becomes corrupted somehow, you can just delete the `.julia` folder, enter `Pkg.init()`, and start with an empty cache. Then, add the packages you need.

Adding a new package

Before adding a new package, it is always a good idea to update your package database for the already installed packages with the Pkg.update() command. Then, add a new package by issuing the Pkg.add("PackageName") command, and execute using PackageName in code or in the REPL. For example, to add 2D plotting capabilities, install the Winston package with Pkg.add("Winston "). To make a graph of 100 random numbers between 0 and 1, execute the following commands:

```
using Winston
plot(rand(100))
```

The rand(100) function is an array with 100 random numbers. This produces the following output:

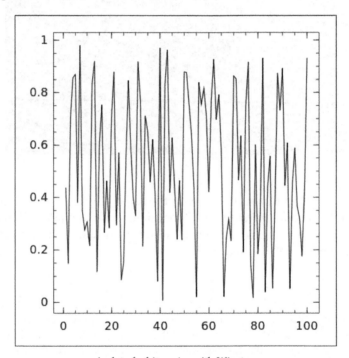

A plot of white noise with Winston

After installing a new Julia version, update all the installed packages by running Pkg.update() in the REPL. For more detailed information, you can refer to http://docs.julialang.org/en/latest/manual/packages/.

Installing and working with Julia Studio

Julia Studio is a free desktop app for working with Julia that runs on Linux, Windows, and OS X (http://forio.com/labs/julia-studio/). It works with the 0.3 release on Windows (Version 0.2.1 for Linux and OS X, at this time, if you want Julia Studio to work with Julia v0.3 on Linux and OS X, you have to do the compilation of the source code of the Studio yourself). It contains a sophisticated editor and integrated REPL, version control with Git, and a very handy side pane with access to the command history, filesystem, packages, and the list of edited documents. It is created by *Forio*, a company that makes software for simulations, data explorations, interactive learning, and predictive analytics. In the following screenshot, you can see some of Julia Studio's features, such as the **Console** section and the green **Run** button (or *F5*) in the upper-right corner. The simple program fizzbuzz.jl prints for the first 100 integers for "fizz" if the number is a multiple of 3, "buzz" if a multiple of 5, and "fizzbuzz" if it is a multiple of 15.

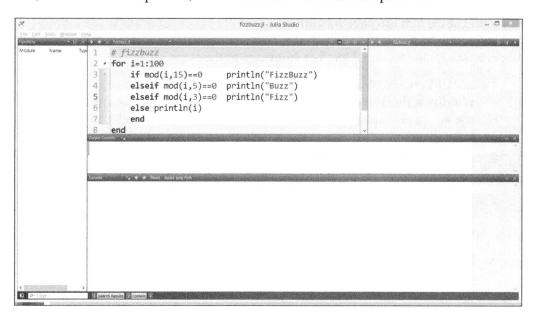

Julia Studio

Notice the # sign that indicates the beginning of comments, the elegant and familiar for loop and if elseif construct, and how they are closed with end. The 1:100 range is a range; mod returns the remainder of the division; the function mod(i, n) can also be written as an i % n operator. Using four spaces for indentation is a convention. Recently, Forio also developed Epicenter, a computational platform for hosting the server-side models (also in Julia), and building interactive web interfaces for these models.

Installing and working with IJulia

IJulia (https://github.com/JuliaLang/IJulia.jl) is a combination of the IPython web frontend interactive environment (http://ipython.org/) with a Julia-language backend. It allows you to work with IPython's powerful graphical notebook (which combines code, formatted text, math, and multimedia in a single document) with qtconsole and regular REPL. Detailed instructions for installation are found at the GitHub page for IJulia (https://github.com/JuliaLang/IJulia.jl) and in the *Julia at MIT* notes (https://github.com/stevengj/julia-mit/blob/master/README.md). Here is a summary of the steps:

1. Install Version 1.0 or later of IPython via easy_install or pip (on OS X and Windows, this is included in the Anaconda Python installation). On Linux, use apt-get install ipython. (For more information, refer to the IPython home page).

2. Install PyQt4 or PySide for qtconsole.

3. Install the IJulia package from the REPL with Pkg.add("IJulia").

4. Install the PyPlot package with Pkg.add("PyPlot").

You can work with IJulia in either of two ways:

- Start an IPython notebook in your web browser by typing the following command in a console:

```
ipython notebook --profile julia
```

- Start qtconsole with:

```
ipython qtconsole --profile Julia
```

The IJulia dashboard on Ubuntu

Verify that you have started IJulia. You must see IJ and the Julia logo in the upper-left corner of the browser window. Julia code is entered in the input cells (input can be multiline) and then executed with *Shift + Enter*. Here is a small example:

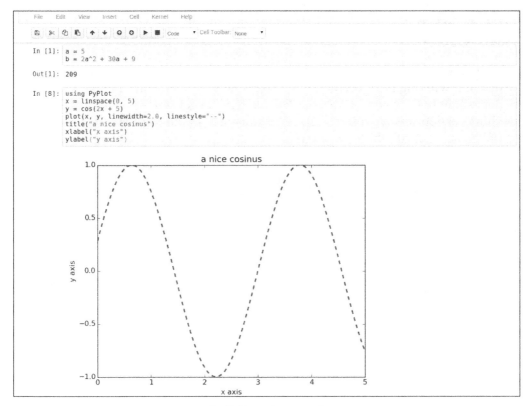

An IJulia session example

In the first input cell, the value of b is calculated from a:

```
a = 5
b = 2a^2 + 30a + 9
```

In the second input cell, we use `PyPlot` (this requires the installation of `matplotlib`; for example, on Linux, this is done by `sudo apt-get install python-matplotlib`).

The `linspace(0, 5)` command defines an array of 100 equally spaced values between `0` and `5`, y is defined as a function of x and is then shown graphically with the plot as follows:

```
using PyPlot
x = linspace(0, 5)
y = cos(2x + 5)
plot(x, y, linewidth=2.0, linestyle="--")
title("a nice cosinus")
xlabel("x axis")
ylabel("y axis")
```

Save a notebook in file format (with the extension `.ipynb`) by downloading it from the menu. If working in an IPython notebook is new for you, you can take a look at the demo at `http://ipython.org/notebook.html` to get started. After installing a new Julia version, always run `Pkg.build("IJulia")` in the REPL in order to rebuild the IJulia package with this new version.

Installing Sublime-IJulia

The popular Sublime Text editor (`http://www.sublimetext.com/3`) now has a plugin based on IJulia (`https://github.com/quinnj/Sublime-IJulia`) authored by Jacob Quinn. It gives you syntax highlighting, autocompletion, and an in-editor REPL, which you basically just open like any other text file, but it runs Julia code for you. You can also select some code from a code file and send it to the REPL with the shortcut *CTRL + B*, or send the entire file there. Sublime-IJulia provides a frontend to the IJulia backend kernel, so that you can start an IJulia frontend in a Sublime view and interact with the kernel. Here is a summary of the installation, for details you can refer to the preceding URL:

1. From within the Julia REPL, install the ZMQ and IJulia packages.
2. From within Sublime Text, install the Package Control package (`https://sublime.wbond.net/installation`).

3. From within Sublime Text, install the `IJulia` package from the Sublime command palette.

4. *Ctrl + Shift + P* opens up a new IJulia console. Start entering commands, and press *Shift + Enter* to execute them. The *Tab* key provides command completion.

Installing Juno

Another promising IDE for Julia and a work in progress by Mike Innes and Keno Fisher is **Juno**, which is based on the Light Table environment. The docs at `http://junolab.org/docs/installing.html` provides detailed instructions for installing and configuring Juno. Here is a summary of the steps:

1. Get LightTable from `http://lighttable.com`.

2. Start LightTable, install the `Juno` plugin through its plugin manager, and restart LightTable.

Light Table works extensively with a command palette that you can open by typing *Ctrl + SPACE*, entering a command, and then selecting it. Juno provides an integrated console, and you can evaluate single expressions in the code editor directly by typing *Ctrl + Enter* at the end of the line. A complete script is evaluated by typing *Ctrl + Shift + Enter*.

Other editors and IDEs

For terminal users, the available editors are as follows:

- **Vim** together with `Julia-vim` works great (`https://github.com/JuliaLang/julia-vim`)
- **Emacs** with `julia-mode.el` from the `https://github.com/JuliaLang/julia/tree/master/contrib` directory

On Linux, **gedit** is very good. The Julia plugin works well and provides autocompletion. **Notepad++** also has Julia support from the `contrib` directory mentioned earlier.

The **SageMath** project (`https://cloud.sagemath.com/`) runs Julia in the cloud within a terminal and lets you work with IPython notebooks. You can also work and teach with Julia in the cloud using the **JuliaBox** platform (`https://juliabox.org/`).

How Julia works

(You can safely skip this section on a first reading.)

Julia works with an LLVM JIT compiler framework that is used for just-in-time generation of machine code. The first time you run a Julia function, it is parsed and the types are inferred. Then, LLVM code is generated by the **JIT (just-in-time)** compiler, which is then optimized and compiled down to native code. The second time you run a Julia function, the native code already generated is called. This is the reason why, the second time you call a function with arguments of a specific type, it takes much less time to run than the first time (keep this in mind when doing benchmarks of Julia code). This generated code can be inspected. Suppose, for example, we have defined a f(x) = 2x + 5 function in a REPL session. Julia responds with the message, **f (generic function with 1 method)**; the code is *dynamic* because we didn't have to specify the type of x or f. Functions are by default *generic* because they are ready to work with different data types for their variables. The code_llvm function can be used to see the JIT bytecode, for example, the version where the x argument is of type Int64:

```
julia> code_llvm(f, (Int64,))

define i64 @"julia_f;1065"(i64) {
top:
  %1 = shl i64 %0, 1, !dbg !3248
  %2 = add i64 %1, 5, !dbg !3248
  ret i64 %2, !dbg !3248
}
```

The code_native function can be used to see the assembly code generated for the same type of x:

```
julia> code_native(f, (Int64,))
        .text
Filename: none
Source line: 1
        push    RBP
        mov     RBP, RSP
Source line: 1
        lea     RAX, QWORD PTR [RCX + RCX + 5]
        pop     RBP
        ret
```

Compare this with the code generated when x is of type Float64:

```
julia> code_native(f, (Float64,))
        .text
Filename: none
Source line: 1
        push    RBP
        mov     RBP, RSP
Source line: 1
        vaddsd  XMM0, XMM0, XMM0
        movabs  RAX, 48532256
        vaddsd  XMM0, XMM0, QWORD PTR [RAX]
        pop     RBP
        ret
```

Julia code is fast because it generates specialized versions of functions for each data type. Julia implements automatic memory management. The user doesn't have to worry about allocating and keeping track of the memory for specific objects. Automatic deletion of objects that are not needed any more (and hence, reclamation of the memory associated with those objects) is done using a garbage collector (GC). The garbage collector runs at the same time as your program. Exactly when a specific object is garbage collected is unpredictable. In Version 0.3, the GC is a simple mark-and-sweep garbage collector; this will change to an incremental mark-and-sweep GC in Version 0.4. You can start garbage collection yourself by calling gc(), or if it runs in the way you can disable it by calling gc_disable().

The standard library is implemented in Julia itself. The I/O functions rely on the libuv library for efficient, platform-independent I/O. The standard library is also contained in a package called Base, which is automatically imported when starting Julia.

Summary

By now, you should have been able to install Julia in a working environment you prefer. You should also have some experience with working in the REPL. We will put this to good use starting in the next chapter, where we will meet the basic data types in Julia, by testing out everything in the REPL.

2
Variables, Types, and Operations

Julia is an optionally typed language, which means that the user can choose to specify the type of arguments passed to a function and the type of variables used inside a function. Julia's type system is the key for its performance; understanding it well is important, and it can pay to use type annotations, not only for documentation or tooling, but also for execution speed. This chapter discusses the realm of elementary built-in types in Julia, the operations that can be performed on them as well as the important concepts of types and scope.

The following topics are covered in this chapter:

- Variables, naming conventions, and comments
- Types
- Integers
- Floating point numbers
- Elementary mathematical functions and operations
- Rational and complex numbers
- Characters
- Strings
- Regular expressions
- Ranges and arrays
- Dates and times
- Scope and constants

You will need to follow along by typing in the examples in the REPL, or executing the code snippets in the code files of this chapter.

Variables, naming conventions, and comments

Data is stored in *values* such as 1, 3.14, "Julia", and every value has a *type*, for example, the type of 3.14 is Float64. Some other examples of elementary values and their data types are 42 of the Int64 type, true and false of the Bool type, and 'X' of the Char type.

Julia, unlike many modern programming languages, differentiates between single characters and strings. Strings can contain any number of characters and are specified using double quotes, and single quotes are only used for character literals. Variables are the names that are *bound* to values by assignments, such as x = 42. They have the type of the value they contain (or reference); this type is given by the typeof function. For example, typeof(x) returns Int64.

The type of a variable can change, because putting x = "I am Julia" now results in typeof(x) returning ASCIIString. In Julia, we don't have to declare a variable (that indicates its type) such as in C or Java for instance, but a variable must be *initialized* (that is bound to a value), so that Julia can deduce its type.

```
julia> y = 7
7
typeof(y)    # Int64
julia> y + z
ERROR: z not defined
```

In the preceding example, z was not assigned a value before using it, so we got an error. By combining variables through operators and functions such as the + operator (as in the preceding example), we get **expressions**. An expression always results in a new value after computation. Contrary to many other languages, *everything in Julia is an expression*, so it returns a value. That's why working in a REPL is so great because you can see the values at each step.

The type of variables determines what you can do with them, that is, the operators with which they can be combined, in this sense, Julia is a *strongly-typed language*. In the following example, x is still a String value, so it can't be summed with y which is of type Int64, but if we give x a float value, the sum can be calculated, as shown in the following example:

```
julia> x + y
ERROR: `+` has no method matching +(::ASCIIString, ::Int64)
julia> x = 3.5; x + y
10.5
```

Here, the semicolon (;) ends the first expression and suppresses its output. Names of the variables are case sensitive. By convention, lower case is used with multiple words separated by an underscore. They start with a letter and after that, you can use letters, digits, underscores, and exclamation points. You can also use Unicode characters. Use clear, short, and to the point names. Here are some valid variable names: `mass`, `moon_velocity`, `current_time`, `pos3`, and `ω1`. However, the last two are not very descriptive, and they could better be replaced with, for example, `particle_position` and `particle_ang_velocity`.

A line of code preceded by a hash sign (#) is a comment, as we can see in the following example:

```
# Calculate the gravitational acceleration grav_acc:
gc = 6.67e-11 # gravitational constant in m3/kg s2
mass_earth = 5.98e24   # in kg
radius_earth = 6378100 # in m
grav_acc = gc * mass_earth / radius_earth^2 # 9.8049 m/s2
```

Multi-line comments are helpful for writing comments that span across multiple lines or commenting out code. Julia will treat all the text between #= and =# as a comment. For printing out values, use the `print` or `println` functions as follows:

```
julia> print(x)
3.5
```

If you want your printed output to be in color, use `print_with_color(:red, "I love Julia!")` that returns the argument string in the color indicated by the first argument.

The term object (or instance) is frequently used when dealing with variables of more complex types. However, we will see that when doing actions on objects, Julia uses functional semantics. We write `action(object)` instead of `object.action()`, as we do in more object-oriented languages such as Java or C#.

In a REPL, the value of the last expression is automatically displayed each time a statement is evaluated (unless it ends with a ; sign). In a standalone script, Julia will not display anything unless the script specifically instructs it to. This is achieved with a `print` or `println` statement. To display any object in the way the REPL does in code, use `display(object)`.

Types

Julia's type system is unique. Julia behaves as a dynamically-typed language (such as Python for instance) most of the time. This means that a variable bound to an integer at one point might later be bound to a string. For example, consider the following:

```
julia> x = 10
10
julia> x = "hello"
"hello"
```

However, one can, optionally, add type information to a variable. This causes the variable to only accept values that match that specific type. This is done through a type annotation. For instance, declaring `x::ASCIIString` implies that only strings can be bound to `x`; in general, it looks like `var::TypeName`. These are used most often to qualify the arguments a function can take. The extra type information is useful for documenting the code, and often allows the JIT compiler to generate better optimized native code. It also allows the development environments to give more support, and code tools such as a linter that can check your code for possible wrong type use.

Here is an example: a function with the `calc_position` name defined as the function `calc_position(time::Float64)`, indicates that this function takes one argument named `time` of the type `Float64`.

Julia uses the same syntax for type assertions that are used to check whether a variable or an expression has a specific type. Writing `(expr)::TypeName` raises an error if `expr` is not of the required type. For instance, consider the following:

```
julia> (2+3)::ASCIIString
ERROR: type: typeassert: expected ASCIIString, got Int64
```

Notice that the type comes after the variable name, unlike in most other languages. In general, the type of a variable can change in Julia, but this is detrimental to performance. For utmost performance, you need to write type-stable code. Code is type-stable if the type of every variable does not vary over time. Carefully thinking in terms of the types of variables is useful in avoiding performance bottlenecks. Adding type annotations to variables updated in the inner loop of a critical region of code can lead to drastic improvements in the performance by helping the JIT compiler remove some type checking. To see an excellent example where this is important, read the article available at `http://www.johnmyleswhite.com/notebook/2013/12/06/writing-type-stable-code-in-julia/`.

A lot of types exist, in fact, a whole type hierarchy is built in in Julia. If you don't specify the type of a function argument, it has the type `Any`, which is effectively the root or parent of all types. Every object is at least of the universal type `Any`. At the other end of the spectrum, there is type `None` that has no values. No object can have this type, but it is a subtype of every other type. While running the code, Julia will infer the type of the parameters passed in a function, and with this information, it will generate optimal machine code.

You can define your own custom types as well, for instance, a `Person` type. By convention, the names of types begin with a capital letter, and if necessary, the word separation is shown with CamelCase, such as `BigFloat` or `AbstractArray`.

If `x` is a variable, then `typeof(x)` gives its type, and `isa(x, T)` tests whether x is of type `T`. For example, `isa("ABC", String)` returns `true`, and `isa(1, Bool)` returns `false`.

Everything in Julia has a type, including types themselves, which are of type `DataType`: `typeof(Int64)` returns `DataType`. Conversion of a variable `var` to a type `Type1` can be done using the type name (lower-cased) as a function `type1(var)`, for example, `int64(3.14)` returns `3`.

However, this raises an error if type conversion is impossible as follows:

```
julia> int64("hello")
ERROR: invalid base 10 digit 'h' in "hello"
```

Integers

Julia offers support for integer numbers ranging from types `Int8` to `Int128`, with `8` to `128` representing the number of bits used, and with unsigned variants with a `U` prefix, such as `UInt8`. The default type (which can also be used as `Int`) is `Int32` or `Int64` depending on the target machine architecture. The bit width is given by the variable `WORD_SIZE`. The number of bits used by the integer affects the maximum and minimum value this integer can have. The minimum and maximum values are given by the functions `typemin()` and `typemax()` respectively, for example, `typemax(Int16)` returns `32767`.

If you try to store a number larger than that allowed by `typemax`, *overflow* occurs. For example:

```
julia> typemax(Int)
9223372036854775807 # might be different on 32 bit platform
julia> ans + 1
-9223372036854775808
```

Overflow checking is not automatic, so an explicit check (for example, the result has the wrong sign) is needed when this can occur. Integers can also be written in binary (`0b`), octal (`0o`), and hexadecimal (`0x`) format.

For computations needing arbitrary-precision integers, Julia has a `BigInt` type. These values can be constructed as `BigInt("number")`, and support the same operators as normal integers. Conversions between numeric types are automatic, but not between the primitive types and the `Big-` types. The normal operations of addition (`+`), subtraction (`-`), and multiplication (`*`) apply for integers. A division (`/`) always gives a floating point number. If you only want integer divisor and remainder, use `div` and `rem`. The symbol `^` is used to obtain the power of a number. The logical values, `true` and `false`, of type `Bool` are also integers with 8 bits. `0` amounts to `false`, and `1` (in fact, also all values other than `0`) to `true`; for example, `bool(-56)` returns `true`. Negation can be done with the `!` operator; for example, `!true` is `false`. Comparing numbers with `==` (equal), `!=` or `<` and `>` return a `Bool` value, and comparisons can be chained after one another (as in `0 < x < 3`).

Floating point numbers

Floating point numbers follow the IEEE 754 standard and represent numbers with a decimal point such as `3.14` or an exponent notation `4e-14`, and come in the types `Float16` up to `Float64`, the last one used for double precision.

Single precision is achieved through the use of the `Float32` type. Single precision float literals must be written in scientific notation, such as `3.14f0`, but with `f` ,where one normally uses `e`. That is, `2.5f2` indicates `2.5*10^2` with single precision, while `2.5e2` indicates `2.5*10^2` in double precision. Julia also has a `BigFloat` type for arbitrary-precision floating numbers' computations.

A built-in type promotion system takes care of all the numeric types that can work together seamlessly, so that there is no explicit conversion needed. Special values exist: `Inf` and `-Inf` for infinity, and `NaN` is used for "not a number"-values such as the result of `0/0` or `Inf - Inf`.

Floating point arithmetic in all programming languages is often a source of subtle bugs and counter-intuitive behavior. For instance:

```
julia> 0.1 + 0.2
0.30000000000000000004
```

This happens because of the way the floating point numbers are stored internally. Most numbers cannot be stored internally with a finite number of bits, such as 1/3 has no finite representation in base 10. The computer will choose the closest number it can represent, introducing a small **round off error**. These errors might accumulate over the course of long computations, creating subtle problems.

Maybe the most important consequence of this is the need to avoid using equality when comparing floating point numbers:

```
julia> 0.1 + 0.2 == 0.3
false
```

A better solution is to use `>=` or `<=` comparisons in Boolean tests that involve floating point numbers, wherever possible.

Elementary mathematical functions and operations

You can view the binary representation of any number (integer or float) with the `bits` function, for example, `bits(3)` returns "00000000000000000000000000000000 0000000000000000000000000000000011".

To round a number, use the `round()` or `iround()` functions: the first returns a floating point number, and the last returns an integer. All standard mathematical functions are provided, such as `sqrt()`, `cbrt()`, `exp()`, `log()`, `sin()`, `cos()`, `tan()`, `erf()` (the error function), and many more (refer to the following URL). To generate a random number, use `rand()`.

Use parentheses `( )` around expressions to enforce precedence. Chained assignments such as `a = b = c = d = 1` are allowed. The assignments are evaluated right-to-left. Assignments for different variables can be combined, as shown in the following example:

```
a = 1; b = 2; c = 3; d = 4
a, b = c, d
```

Now, a has value 3 and b has value 4. In particular, this makes an easy swap possible:

```
a, b = b, a    # now a is 4 and b is 3
```

Like in many other languages, the Boolean operators work on the `true` and `false` values for and, or, and not have as symbols `&&`, `||`, and `!` respectively. Julia applies a short-circuit optimization here. That means:

- In `a && b`, `b` is not evaluated when `a` is false (since `&&` is already false)
- In `a || b`, `b` is not evaluated when `a` is true (since `||` is already true)

The operators `&` and `|` are also used for non-short-circuit Boolean evaluations.

Julia also supports bitwise operations on integers. Note that `n++` or `n--` with `n` as an integer does not exist in Julia, as it does in C++ or Java. Use `n += 1` or `n -= 1` instead.

For more detailed information on operations, such as the bitwise operators, special precedence, and so on, refer to `http://docs.julialang.org/en/latest/manual/mathematical-operations/`.

Rational and complex numbers

Julia supports these types out of the box. The global constant `im` represents the square root of `-1`, so that `3.2 + 7.1im` is a complex number with floating point coefficients, so it is of the type `Complex{Float64}`.

This is the first example of a **parametric type** in Julia. For this example, we can write this as `Complex{T}`, where type `T` can take a number of different type values such as `Int32` or `Int64`.

All operations and elementary functions such as `exp()`, `sqrt()`, `sinh()`, `real()`, `imag()`, `abs()`, and so on are also defined on complex numbers; for example, `abs(3.2 + 7.1im) = 7.787810988975015`.

If `a` and `b` are two variables that contain a number, use `complex(a,b)` to form a complex number with them. Rational numbers are useful when you want to work with exact ratios of integers, for example, `3//4`, which is of type `Rational{Int64}`. Again, comparisons and standard operations are defined: `float()` converts to a floating point number, and `num()` and `denum()` gives the numerator and denominator. Both types work together seamlessly with all the other numeric types.

Characters

Like C or Java, but unlike Python, Julia implements a type for a single character, the Char type. A character literal is written as 'A', typeof('A') returns Char. A Char type is, in fact, a 32-bit integer whose numeric value is a Unicode code point, and they range from '\0' to '\Uffffffff'. Convert this to its code point with int(): int('A') returns 65, int('α') returns 945, so this takes two bytes.

The reverse also works: char(65) returns 'A', char(945) returns '\u3b1', the code point for α (3b1 is hexadecimal for 945).

Unicode characters can be entered by a \u in single quotes, followed by four hexadecimal digits (0-9, A-F), or \U followed by eight hexadecimal digits. The function is_valid_char() can test whether a number returns an existing Unicode character: is_valid_char(0x3b1) returns true. The normal escape characters such as \t (tab), \n (newline), \', and so on also exist in Julia.

Strings

Literal strings are always ASCII (if they only contain ASCII letters) or UTF8 (if they contain characters that cannot be represented in ASCII), as in this example:

```
julia> typeof("hello")
ASCIIString
julia> typeof("Güdrun")
UTF8String
```

UTF16 and UTF32 are also supported. Strings are contained in double quotes (" ") or triple quotes (''' '''). They are immutable, which means that they cannot be altered once they have been defined:

```
julia> s = "Hello, Julia"
julia> s[2] = "z"
ERROR: 'setindex!' has no method matching setindex!...
```

A String is a succession, or an array of characters (see the *Ranges and arrays* section) that can be extracted from the string by indexing it, starting from 1: with str = "Julia", then str[1] returns the Char 'J', and str[end] returns the Char 'a', the last character in the string. The index of the last byte is also given by endof(str), and length() returns the number of characters. These two are different if the string contains multi-byte Unicode characters, for example, endof("Güdrun") gives 7, while length("Güdrun") gives 6.

Using an index less than one or greater than the index of the last byte gives `BoundsError`. In general, strings can contain Unicode characters, which can take up to four bytes, so not every index is a valid character index. For example, for `str2 = "I am the α: the beginning"`, we have `str2[10]` that returns `'\u3b1'` (the two-byte character representing α), `str2[11]` returns `ERROR: invalid UTF-8 character index` (because this is the second byte of the α character) and `str2[12]` returns colon (`:`).

We see 25 characters, `length(str2)` returns 25, but the last index given by `endof(str2)` returns 26. For this reason, looping over a string's characters can best be done as an iteration and not using the index, as follows:

```
for c in str2
    println(c)
end
```

A substring can be obtained by taking a range of indices: `str[3:5]` or `str[3:end]` returns `"lia"`. A string that contains a single Char is different from that Char value: `'A' == "A"` returns `false`.

Julia has an elegant string interpolation mechanism for constructing strings: `$var` inside a string is replaced by the value of `var`, and `$(expr)`, where `expr` is an expression, is replaced by its computed value. When a is 2 and b is 3, the following expression `"$a * $b = $(a * b)"` returns `"2 * 3 = 6"`. If you need to write the $ sign in a string, escape it as `\$`.

You can also concatenate strings with the `*` operator or with the `string()` function: `"ABC" * "DEF"` returns `"ABCDEF"`, and `string("abc", "def", "ghi")` returns `"abcdefghi"`.

Strings prefixed with `:` are of type `Symbol`, such as `:green`; we already used it in the `print_with_color` function. They are more efficient than strings and are used for IDs or keys. Symbols cannot be concatenated. They should only be used if they are expected to remain constant over the course of the execution of the program. The `String` type is very rich, and it has 354 functions defined on it, given by `methodswith(String)`. Some useful methods include:

- `search(string, char)`: This returns the index of the first matching char in string, or the range of a substring: `search("Julia",'l')` returns 3.

- `replace(string, str1, str2)`: This changes substrings str1 to str2 in string, for example, `replace("Julia","u", "o")` returns `"Jolia"`.

- `split(string, char or [chars])`: This splits a string on the specified char or chars, for example, `split("34,Tom Jones,Pickwick Street 10,Aberdeen", ',')` returns the four strings in an array: `["34","Tom Jones","Pickwick Street 10","Aberdeen"]`; if char is not specified, the split is done on space characters (spaces, tabs, newlines, and so on).

Formatting numbers and strings

The `@printf` macro (we'll look deeper into macros in *Chapter 7, Metaprogramming in Julia*) takes a format string and one or more variables to substitute into this string while being formatted. It works in a manner similar to `printf` in C. You can write a format string that includes placeholders for variables. For example:

```
julia> name = "Pascal"

julia> @printf("Hello, %s \n", name) # returns Hello, Pascal
```

If you need a string as the return value, use the macro `@sprintf`.

The following `chapter 2\formatting.jl` script shows the most common formats (`show` is a basic function that prints a text representation of an object, often more specific than `print`):

```
# d for integers:
@printf("%d\n", 1e5) #> 100000
x = 7.35679
# f = float format, rounded if needed:
@printf("x = %0.3f\n", x) #> 7.357
aa = 1.5231071779744345
bb = 33.976886930000695
@printf("%.2f %.2f\n", aa, bb) #> 1.52 33.98
# or to create another string:
str = @sprintf("%0.3f", x)
show(str) #> "7.357"
println()
# e = scientific format with e:
@printf("%0.6e\n", x) #> 7.356790e+00
# c = for characters:
@printf("output: %c\n", 'α') #> output: α
# s for strings:
@printf("%s\n", "I like Julia")
# right justify:
@printf("%50s\n", "text right justified!")
```

The following output is obtained on running the preceding script:

```
100000
x = 7.357
1.52 33.98
"7.357"
7.356790e+00
output: α
I like Julia
            text right justified!
```

A special kind of string is `VersionNumber` that takes the form `v"0.3.0"` (note the preceding v), with optional additional details. They can be compared, and are used for Julia's versions, but also in the package versions and dependency mechanism of `Pkg` (refer to the *Packages* section of *Chapter 1, Installing the Julia Platform*). If you have the code that works differently for different versions, use something as follows:

```
if v"0.3" <= VERSION < v"0.4-"
# do something specific to 0.3 release series
end
```

Regular expressions

To search for and match patterns in text and other data, regular expressions are an indispensable tool for the data scientist. Julia adheres to the Perl syntax of regular expressions. For a complete reference, refer to `http://www.regular-expressions.info/reference.html`. Regular expressions are represented in Julia as a double (or triple) quoted string preceded by `r`, such as `r"..."` (optionally, followed by one or more of the i, s, m, or x flags), and they are of type `Regex`. The `chapter 2\regexp.jl` script shows some examples.

In the first example, we will match the e-mail addresses (`#>` shows the result):

```
email_pattern = r".+@.+"
input = "john.doe@mit.edu"
println(ismatch(email_pattern, input)) #> true
```

The regular expression pattern + matches any (non-empty) group of characters. Thus, this pattern matches any string that contains @ somewhere in the middle.

In the second example, we will try to determine whether a credit card number is valid or not:

```
visa = r"^(?:4[0-9]{12}(?:[0-9]{3})?)$"  # the pattern
input = "4457418557635128"
ismatch(visa, input)  #> true
if ismatch(visa, input)
    println("credit card found")
    m = match(visa, input)
    println(m.match) #> 4457418557635128
    println(m.offset) #> 1
    println(m.offsets) #> []
end
```

The function `ismatch(regex, string)` returns `true` or `false`, depending on whether the given `regex` matches the string, so we can use it in an if expression. If you want the detailed information of the pattern matching, use `match` instead of `ismatch`. This either returns `nothing` when there is no match, or an object of type `RegexMatch` when the pattern is found (`nothing` is, in fact, a value to indicate that nothing is returned or printed, and it has type `Nothing`).

The `RegexMatch` object has the following properties:

- `match` contains the entire substring that matches (in this example, it contains the complete number)

- `offset` tells at what position the matching begins (here, it is 1)

- `offsets` gives the same information as the preceding line, but for each of the captured substrings

- `captures` contains the captured substrings as a tuple (refer to the following example)

Besides, checking whether a string matches a particular pattern, regular expressions can also be used to *capture* parts of the string. We do this by enclosing parts of the pattern in parentheses `( )`. For instance, to capture the username and hostname in the e-mail address pattern used earlier, we modify the pattern as:

```
email_pattern = r"(.+)@(.+)"
```

Notice how the characters before @ are enclosed in brackets. This tells the regular expression engine that we want to capture this specific set of characters. To see how this works, consider the following example:

```
email_pattern = r"(.+)@(.+)"
input = "john.doe@mit.edu"
m = match(email_pattern, input)
println(m.captures) #> ["john.doe","mit.edu"]
```

Here is another example:

```
m = match(r"(ju|l)(i)?(a)", "Julia")
println(m.match) #> "lia"
println(m.captures) #> l - i - a
println(m.offset) #> 3
println(m.offsets) #> 3 - 4 - 5
```

The `search` and `replace` functions also take regular expressions as arguments, for example, `replace("Julia", r"u[\w]*l", "red")` returns `"Jredia"`. If you want to work with all the matches, `matchall` and `eachmatch` come in handy:

```
str = "The sky is blue"
reg = r"[\w]{3,}" # matches words of 3 chars or more
r = matchall(reg, str)
show(r) #> ["The","sky","blue"]
iter = eachmatch(reg, str)
for i in iter
    println("\"$(i.match)\" ")
end
```

The `matchall` function returns an array with `RegexMatch` for each match. `eachmatch` returns an iterator `iter` over all the matches, which we can loop through with a simple for loop. The screen output is `"The"`, `"sky"`, and `"blue"` printed on consecutive lines.

Ranges and arrays

When we execute `search("Julia", "uli")`, the result is not an index number, but a range `2:4` that indicates the index interval for the searched substring. This comes in handy when you have to work with an interval of numbers, for example, one up to thousand: `1:1000`. The type of this object `typeof(1:1000)` is `UnitRange{Int64}`. By default, the step is `1`, but this can also be specified as the second number; `0:5:100` gives all multiples of 5 up to 100. You can iterate over a range as follows:

```
# code from file chapter2\arrays.jl
for i in 1:2:9

    println(i)
end
```

This prints out 1 3 5 7 9 on consecutive lines.

In the previous section on Strings, we already encountered the Array type when discussing the `split` function:

```
a = split("A,B,C,D",",")
typeof(a) #> Array{SubString{ASCIIString},1}
show(a) #> SubString{ASCIIString}["A","B","C","D"]
```

Julia's arrays are very efficient, powerful, and flexible. The general type format for an array is `Array{Type, n}`, with n number of dimensions (we will discuss multidimensional arrays or matrices in *Chapter 5, Collection Types*). As with the complex type, we can see that the `Array` type is generic, and all the elements have to be of the same type. A one-dimensional array (also called a **Vector** in Julia) can be initialized by separating its values by commas and enclosing them in square brackets, for example, `arr = [100, 25, 37]` is a 3-element `Array{Int64,1}`; the type is automatically inferred with this notation. If you want explicitly the type to be `Any`, then define it as follows: `arra = Any[100, 25, "ABC"]`. Notice that we don't have to indicate the number of elements. Julia takes care of that and lets an array grow dynamically when needed.

Arrays can also be constructed by passing a type parameter and number of elements:

```
arr2 = Array(Int64,5) # is a 5-element Array{Int64,1}

show(arr2) #> [0,0,0,0,0]
```

When making an array like this, you cannot be sure that it will be initialized to 0 values (refer to the *Other ways to create arrays* section to learn how to initialize an array).

You can define an array with 0 elements of type `Float64` as follows:

```
arr3 = Float64[] #> 0-element Array{Float64,1}
```

To populate this array, use `push!`; for example, `push!(arr3, 1.0)` returns 1-element `Array{Float64,1}`.

Creating an empty array with `arr3 = []` is not very useful because the element type is `Any`. Julia wants to be able to infer the type!

Arrays can also be initialized from a range:

```
arr4 = [1:7] #> 7-element Array{Int64,1}: [1,2,3,4,5,6,7]
```

Of course, when dealing with large arrays, it is better to indicate the final number of elements from the start for the performance. Suppose you know beforehand that `arr2` will need 10^5 elements, but not more. If you do `sizehint(arr2, 10^5)`, you'll be able to `push!` at least 10^5 elements without Julia having to reallocate and copy the data already added, leading to a substantial improvement in performance.

Arrays store a sequence of values of the same type (called elements), indexed by integers 1 through the number of elements (as in mathematics, but unlike most other high-level languages such as Python). As with strings, we can access the individual elements with the bracket notation; for example, with `arr` being `[100, 25, 37]`, `arr[1]` returns `100`, and `arr[end]` is `37`. Use an invalid index result in an exception as follows:

```
arr[6] #> ERROR: BoundsError()
```

You can also set a specific element the other way around:

```
arr[2] = 5 #> [100, 5, 37]
```

The main characteristics of an array are given by the following functions:

- The element type is given by `eltype(arr)`, in our example, is `Int64`
- The number of elements is given by `length(arr)`, here, `3`
- The number of dimensions is given by `ndims(arr)`, here, `1`
- The number of elements in dimension `n` is given by `size(arr, n)`, here, `size(arr, 1)` returns `3`

It is easy to join the array elements to a string separated by a comma character and a space, for example, with `arr4 = [1:7]`:

```
join(arr4, ", ") #> "1, 2, 3, 4, 5, 6, 7"
```

We can also use this range syntax (called a **slice** as in Python) to obtain subarrays:

```
arr4[1:3] #>#> 3-element array [1, 2, 3]
arr4[4:end] #> 3-element array [4, 5, 6, 7]
```

Slices can be assigned to, with one value or with another array:

```
arr = [1,2,3,4,5]
arr[2:4] = [8,9,10]
println(arr) #> 1 8 9 10 5
```

Other ways to create arrays

For convenience, `zeros(n)` returns an `n` element array with all the elements equal to `0.0`, and `ones(n)` does the same with elements equal to `1.0`.

linspace(start, stop, n) creates a vector of n equally spaced numbers from start to stop, for example:

```
eqa = linspace(0, 10, 5)
show(eqa) #> [0.0,2.5,5.0,7.5,10.0]
```

You can use cell to create an array with undefined values: cell(4) creates a four element array {Any,1} with four #undef values as shown:

```
{#undef,#undef,#undef,#undef}
```

To fill an array arr with the same value for all the elements, use fill!(arr, 42), which returns [42, 42, 42]. To create a five-element array with random Int32 numbers, execute the following:

```
v1 = rand(Int32,5)
5-element Array{Int32,1}:
   905745764
   840462491
  -227765082
  -286641110
       16698998
```

To convert this to an array of Int64 elements, just execute int64(v1).

Some common functions for arrays

If b = [1:7] and c = [100,200,300], then you can concatenate b and c with the following command:

```
append!(b, c) #> Now b is [1, 2, 3, 4, 5, 6, 7, 100, 200, 300]
```

The array b is changed by applying this append! method, that's why, it ends in an exclamation mark (!). This is a general convention.

 A function whose name ends in a ! changes its first argument.

Likewise push! and pop! respectively, append one element at the end, or take one away and return that, while the array is changed:

```
pop!(b) #> 300, b is now [1, 2, 3, 4, 5, 6, 7, 100, 200]
push!(b, 42) # b is now [1, 2, 3, 4, 5, 6, 7, 100, 200, 42]
```

If you want to do the same operations on the front of the array, use `shift!` and `unshift!`:

```
shift!(b) #> 1, b is now [2, 3, 4, 5, 6, 7, 100, 200, 42]
unshift!(b, 42) # b is now [42, 2, 3, 4, 5, 6, 7, 100, 200, 42]
```

To remove an element at a certain index, use the `splice!` function as follows:

```
splice!(b,8) #> 100, b is now [42, 2, 3, 4, 5, 6, 7, 200, 42]
```

Checking whether an array contains an element is very easy with the `in` function:

```
in(42, b) #> true , in(43, b) #> false
```

To sort an array, use `sort!`. If you want the array to be changed in place, or `sort` if the original array must stay the same:

```
sort(b) #> [2,3,4,5,6,7,42,42,200], but b is not changed:
println(b) #> [42,2,3,4,5,6,7,200,42]
sort!(b) #>
println(b) #> b is now changed to [2,3,4,5,6,7,42,42,200]
```

To loop over an array, you can use a simple for loop:

```
for e in arr
    print("$e ") # or process e in another way
end
```

If a dot (`.`) precedes operators such as `+` or `*`, the operation is done element wise, that is, on the corresponding elements of the arrays. For example, if `a1 = [1, 2, 3]` and `a2 = [4, 5, 6]`, then `a1 .* a2` returns the array `[4, 10, 18]`. On the other hand, if you want the dot (or scalar) product of vectors, use the `dot(a1, a2)` function ,which returns `32`, so `dot(a1, a2)` gives the same result as `sum(a1 .* a2)`.

Other functions such as `sin()` simply work by applying the operation to each element, for example, `sin(arr)`. Lots of other useful methods exist, such as `repeat([1, 2, 3], inner = [2])`, which produces `[1,1,2,2,3,3]`.

The `methodswith(Array)` function returns 358 methods. You can use `help` in the REPL or search the documentation for more information.

When you assign an array to another array, and then change the first array, both the arrays change. Consider the following example:

```
a = [1,2,4,6]
a1 = a
show(a1) #> [1,2,4,6]
a[4] = 0
```

```
show(a)  #> [1,2,4,0]
show(a1) #> [1,2,4,0]
```

This happens because they point to the same object in memory. If you don't want this, you have to make a copy of the array. Just use b = copy(a) or b = deepcopy(a) if some elements of a are arrays that have to be copied recursively.

As we have seen, arrays are mutable (in contrast to strings) and as arguments to a function they are passed by reference: as a consequence the function can change them, as in this example:

```
a = [1,2,3]
function change_array(arr)
  arr[2] = 25
end
change_array(a)
println(a) #>[ 1, 25, 3]
```

How to convert an array of chars to a string

Suppose you have an array, arr = ['a', 'b', 'c']. Which function on arr do we need to return all characters in one string? The function join will do the trick: join(arr) returns the string "abc"; utf32(arr) does the same thing.

The string(arr) function does not, it returns ['a', 'b', 'c']. However, string(arr...) does return "abc". This is because . . . is the **splice operator** (also known as **splat**) that causes the contents of arr to be passed as individual arguments rather than passing arr as an array.

Dates and times

To get the basic time information, you can use the time() function that returns, for example, 1.408719961424e9, the number of seconds since a predefined date called the epoch (normally, the 1st of January 1970 on Unix system), This is useful for measuring the time interval between two events, for example, to benchmark how long a long calculation takes:

```
start_time = time()
# long computation
time_elapsed = time() - start_time
println("Time elapsed: $time_elapsed")
```

Most useful function is strftime(time()) that returns a string in "22/08/2014 17:06:13" format.

If you want more functionality greater than equal to 0.3 when working in Julia, take a look at the `Dates` package. Add this to the environment with `Pkg.add("Dates")` (it provides a subset of the functionality of the `Dates` module mentioned next). There is also the `Time` package by Quinn Jones. Take a look at the docs to see how to use it (`https://github.com/quinnj/Datetime.jl/wiki/Datetime-Manual`).

Starting from Julia Version 0.4, you should use the `Dates` module built into the standard library, with `Date` for days and `DateTime` for times down to milliseconds. Additional time zone functionality can be added through the `Timezones.jl` package.

The `Date` and `DateTime` functions can be constructed as follows or with simpler versions with less information:

- `d = Date(2014,9,1)` returns `2014-09-01`
- `dt = DateTime(2014,9,1,12,30,59,1)` returns `2014-09-01T12:30:59.001`

These objects can be compared and subtracted to get the duration. `Date` parts or fields can be retrieved through accessor functions, such as `Dates.year(d)`, `Dates.month(d)`, `Dates.week(d)`, and `Dates.day(d)`. Other useful functions exist, such as `dayofweek`, `dayname`, `daysinmonth`, `dayofyear`, `isleapyear`, and so on.

Scope and constants

The region in the program where a variable is known is called the **scope** of that variable. Until now, we have only seen how to create top-level or global variables that are accessible from anywhere in the program. By contrast, variables defined in a local scope can only be used within that scope. A common example of a local scope is the code inside a function. Using global scope variables is not advisable for several reasons, notably the performance. If the value and type can change at any moment in the program, the compiler cannot optimize the code.

So, restricting the scope of a variable to local scope is better. This can be done by defining them within a function or a control construct, as we will see in the following chapters. This way, we can use the same variable name more than once without name conflicts.

Let's take a look at the following code fragment:

```
# code in chapter 2\scope.jl
x = 1.0 # x is Float64
x = 1 # now x is Int
# y::Float64 = 1.0 # LoadError: "y is not defined"
```

```
function scopetest()
    println(x) # 1, x is known here, because it's in global scope
    y::Float64 = 1.0 # y must be Float64, this is not possible in
global scope
end
scopetest()
println(y) #> ERROR: y not defined, only defined in scope of
scopetest()
```

Variable x changes its type, which is allowed, but because it makes the code type-unstable, it could be the source of a performance hit. From the definition of y in the third line, we see that type annotations can only be used in local scope (here, in the scopetest() function).

Some code constructs introduce scope blocks. They support local variables. We have already mentioned functions, but for, while, try, let, and type blocks can all support a local scope. Any variable defined in a for, while, try, or let block will be local unless it is used by an enclosing scope before the block.

The following structure, called a **compound expression**, does not introduce a new scope. Several (preferably short) sub-expressions can be combined in one compound expression if you start it with begin, as in this example:

```
x = begin
  a = 5
  2 * a
end # now x is 10
println(a) #> a is 5
```

After end, x has value 10 and a is 5. This can also be written with ( ) as:

```
x = (a = 5; 2 * a)
```

The value of a compound expression is the value of the last sub-expression. Variables introduced in it are still known after the expression ends.

Values that don't change during program execution are constants, which are declared with const. In other words, they are immutable and their type is inferred. It is a good practice to write their name in uppercase letters, like this:

```
const GC = 6.67e-11 # gravitational constant in m3/kg s2
```

Julia defines a number of constants, such as ARGS (an array that contains the command-line arguments), VERSION (the version of Julia that is running), and OS_NAME (the name of the operating system such as Linux, Windows, or Darwin), mathematical constants (such as pi and e), and datetime constants (such as Friday, Fri, August, and Aug).

If you try to give a global constant a new value, you get a warning, but if you change its type, you get an error as follows:

```
julia> GC = 3.14
     Warning: redefining constant GC
julia> GC = 10
     ERROR: invalid redefinition of constant GC
```

Constants can only be assigned a value once, and their type cannot change, so they can be optimized. Use them whenever possible in the global scope.

So global constants are more about type than value, which makes sense, because Julia gets its speed from knowing the correct types. If, however, the constant variable is of a mutable type (for example, Array, Dict (refer to *Chapter 8, I/O, Networking, and Parallel Computing*)), then you can't change it to a different array, but you can always change the contents of that variable:

```
julia> const ARR = [4,7,1]
julia> ARR[1] = 9
julia> show(ARR) #> [9,7,1]
julia> ARR = [1, 2, 3]
  Warning: redefining constant ARR
```

To review what we have learned in this chapter, we play a bit with characters, strings, and arrays in the following program (strings_arrays.jl):

```
# a newspaper headline:
str = "The Gold and Blue Loses a Bit of Its Luster"
println(str)
nchars = length(str)
println("The headline counts $nchars characters") # 43
str2 = replace(str, "Blue", "Red")
# strings are immutable
println(str) # The Gold and Blue Loses a Bit of Its Luster
println(str2)
println("Here are the characters at position 25 to 30:")
subs = str[25:30]
print("-$(lowercase(subs))-") # "-a bit -"
println("Here are all the characters:")
for c in str
    println(c)
```

```
end
arr = split(str,' ')
show(arr)
#["The","Gold","and","Blue","Loses","a","Bit","of","Its","Luster"]
nwords = length(arr)
println("The headline counts $nwords words") # 10
println("Here are all the words:")
for word in arr
    println(word)
end
arr[4] = "Red"
show(arr) # arrays are mutable
println("Convert back to a sentence:")
nstr = join(arr, ' ')
println(nstr) # The Gold and Red Loses a Bit of Its Luster


# working with arrays:
println("arrays: calculate sum, mean and standard deviation ")
arr = [1:100]
typeof(arr) #>
println(sum(arr)) #> 5050
println(mean(arr)) #> 50.5
println(std(arr)) #> 29.011491975882016
```

Summary

In this chapter, we reviewed some basic elements of Julia, such as constants, variables, and types. We also learned how to work with the basic types such as numbers, characters, strings, and ranges, and encountered the very versatile array type. In the next chapter, we will look in depth at the functions and we will realize that Julia deserves to be called a functional language.

3
Functions

Julia is foremost a functional language because computations and data transformations are done through functions; they are first-class citizens in Julia. Programs are structured around defining functions and to overload them for different combinations of argument types. This chapter discusses this keystone concept, covering the following topics:

- Defining functions
- Optional and keyword arguments
- Anonymous functions
- First-class functions and closures
- Recursive functions
- Map, filter, and list comprehensions
- Generic functions and multiple dispatch

Defining functions

A function is an object that gets a number of arguments (the argument list, `arglist`) as the input, then does something with these values in the function body, and returns none, one, or more value(s). Multiple arguments are separated by commas (,) in `arglist` (in fact, they form a tuple, as do the return values; refer to the *Tuples* section of *Chapter 5*, *Collection Types*). The arguments are also optionally typed, and the type(s) can be user-defined. The general syntax is as follows:

```
function fname(arglist)
    # function body...
    return value(s)
end
```

A function's argument list can also be empty, then it is written as `fname()`.

Here is a simple example:

```
# code in chapter 3\functions101.jl
function mult(x, y)
   println("x is $x and y is $y")
   return x * y
end
```

Function names such as `mult` are by convention in lower case, without underscores. They can contain Unicode characters, which are useful in mathematical notations. The `return` keyword in the last line is optional; we could have written the line as `x * y`. In general, the value of the last expression in the function is returned, but writing `return` is mostly a good idea in multi-line functions to increase the readability.

The function is called with `n = mult(3, 4)` returns `12`, and assigns the `return` value to a new variable n. You can also execute a function just by calling `fname(arglist)` if you only need its side effects (that is, how the function affects the program state; for instance, by changing the global variables). The `return` keyword can also be used within a condition in other parts of the function body to exit the function earlier, as in this example:

```
function mult(x, y)
    println("x is $x and y is $y")
        if x == 1
          return y
        end
    x * y
end
```

In this case, `return` can also be used without a value so that the function returns `nothing`.

Functions are not limited to returning a single value. Here is an example with *multiple return values*:

```
function multi(n, m)
    n*m, div(n,m), n%m
end
```

This returns the tuple (16,4,0) when called with multi(8, 2). The return values can be extracted to other variables such as x, y, z = multi(8, 2), then x becomes 16, y becomes 4, and z becomes 0. In fact, you can say that Julia always returns a single value, but this value can be a tuple that can be used to pass multiple variables back to the program.

We can also have a variable with number of arguments using so-called the varargs function. They are coded as follows:

```
    function varargs(n, m, args...)
     println("arguments : $n $m $args")
end
```

Here, n and m are just positional arguments (there can be more or none at all). The args... argument takes in all the remaining parameters in a tuple. If we call the function with varargs(1, 2, 3, 4), then n is 1, m is 2, and args has the value (3, 4). When there are still more parameters, the tuple can grow, or if there are none, it can be empty ().The same *splat* operator can also be used to unpack a tuple or an array into individual arguments, for example, we can define a second variable argument function as follows:

```
function varargs2(args...)

    println("arguments2: $args")
end
```

With x = (3, 4), we can call varargs2 as varargs2(1, 2, x...). Now, args becomes the tuple (1, 2, 3, 4); the tuple x was *spliced*. This also works for arrays. If x = [10, 11, 12], then args becomes (1, 2, 10, 11, 12). The receiving function does not need to be a variable argument function, but then the number of spliced parameters must exactly match the number of arguments.

It is important to realize that in Julia, all the arguments to functions (with the exception of plain data such as numbers and chars) are passed by reference. Their values are not copied when they are passed, which means they can be changed from inside the function, and the changes will be visible to the calling code.

For example, consider the following code:

```
function insert_elem(arr)
  push!(arr, -10)
end


arr = [2, 3, 4]
insert_elem(arr)
# arr is now [ 2, 3, 4, -10 ]
```

As this example shows, `arr` itself has been modified by the function.

Due to the way Julia compiles, a function must be defined by the time it is actually called (but it can be used before that in other function definitions).

It can also be useful to indicate the argument types to restrict the kind of parameters passed when calling. Our function header for floating point numbers would then look as `function mult(x::Float64, y::Float64)`. When we call this function with `mult(5, 6)`, we receive an error, `ERROR: `mult` has no method matching mult(::Int64, ::Int64)`, proving that Julia is indeed a strongly typed language. It does not accept integer parameters for the floating point arguments.

If we define a function without types, it is generic; the Julia JIT compiler is ready to generate versions called `methods` for different argument types when needed. Define the previous function `mult` in the REPL, and you will see the output as `mult (generic function with 1 method)`.

There is also a more compact, one-line function syntax (the assignment form) for short functions, for example, `mult(x, y) = x * y`. Use this preferably for simple one-line functions, as it will lend the code greater clarity. Because of this, mathematical functions can also be written in an intuitive form: `f(x, y) = x^3 - y + x * y; f(3, 2) #=> 31`.

A function defines its own scope; the set of variables that are declared inside a function are only known inside the function, and this is also true for the arguments. Functions can be defined as top level (global) or nested (a function can be defined within another function). Usually, functions with related functionality are grouped in their own Julia file, which is included in a main file. Or if the function is big enough, it can have its own file, preferably with the same name as the function.

Optional and keyword arguments

When defining functions, one or more arguments can be given a *default* value such as `f(arg = val)`. If no parameter is supplied for `arg`, then `val` is taken as the value of `arg`. The position of these arguments in the function's input is important, just as it is for normal arguments; that's why they are called **optional positional arguments**. Here is an example of a `f` function with an optional argument `b`:

```
# code in chapter 3\arguments.jl:
f(a, b = 5) = a + b
```

If `f(1)`, then it returns `6`, `f(2, 5)` returns `7`, and `f(3)` returns `8`. However, calling it with `f()` or `f(1,2,3)` returns an error, because there is no matching function `f` with zero or three arguments. These arguments are still only defined by position: calling `f(2, b = 5)` raises an error as `ERROR: function f does not accept keyword arguments`.

Until now, arguments were only defined by position. For code clarity, it can be useful to explicitly call the arguments by name, so they are called **optional keyword arguments**. Because the arguments are given explicit names, their order is irrelevant, but they must come last and be separated from the positional arguments by a semi-colon (`;`) in the argument list, as shown in this example:

$$k(x; a1 = 1, a2 = 2) = x * (a1 + a2)$$

Now `k(3, a2 = 3)` returns `12`, `k(3, a2 = 3, a1 = 0)` returns `9` (so their position doesn't matter), but `k(3)` returns `9` (demonstrating that the keyword arguments are optional). Normal, optional positional, and keyword arguments can be combined as follows:

```
function allargs(normal_arg, optional_positional_arg=2; keyword_
arg="ABC")
    print("normal arg: $normal_arg" - )
    print("optional arg: $optional_positional_arg" - )
    print("keyword arg: $keyword_arg")
end
```

If we call `allargs(1, 3, keyword_arg=4)`, it prints `normal arg: 1 - optional arg: 3 - keyword arg: 4`.

A useful case is when the keyword arguments are splatted as follows:

```
function varargs2(;args...)
    args
end
```

Calling this with `varargs2(k1="name1", k2="name2", k3=7)` returns a 3-element `Array{Any,1}` with the elements: `(:k1,"name1")` `(:k2,"name2")` `(:k3,7)`. Now, `args` is a collection of the `(key, value)` tuples, where each key comes from the name of the keyword argument, and it is also a symbol (refer to the *Strings* section of *Chapter 2, Variables, Types, and Operations*) because of the colon (`:`) as prefix.

Anonymous functions

The function `f(x, y)` at the end of the *Defining functions* section can also be written with no name, as an *anonymous* function: `(x, y) -> x^3 - y + x * y`. We can, however, bind it to a name such as `f = (x, y) -> x^3 - y + x * y`, and then call it, for example, as `f(3, 2)`. Anonymous functions are also often written using the following syntax:

```
    function (x)
        x + 2
    end
(anonymous function)
julia> ans(3)
5
```

Often, they are also written with a lambda expression as `(x) -> x + 2`. Before the stab character `"->"` are the arguments, and after the stab character we have the return value. This can be shortened to `x -> x + 2`. A function without arguments would be written as `() -> println("hello, Julia")`.

Here is an anonymous function taking three arguments: `(x, y, z) -> 3x + 2y - z`. When the performance is important, try to use named functions instead, because calling anonymous functions involves a huge overhead. Anonymous functions are mostly used when passing a function as an argument to another function, which is precisely what we will discuss in the next section.

First-class functions and closures

In this section, we will demonstrate the power and flexibility of functions (example code can be found in `chapter 3\first_class.jl`). First, functions have their *own type*: typing `typeof(mult)` in the REPL returns `Function`. Functions can also be *assigned to a variable* by their name:

```
julia> m = mult
julia> m(6, 6) #> 36.
```

This is useful when working with anonymous functions, such as `c = x -> x + 2,` or as follows:

```
julia> plustwo = function (x)
                    x + 2
                end
```

```
(anonymous function)

julia> plustwo(3)

5
```

Operators are just functions written with their arguments in an *infix form*, for example, `x + y` is equivalent to `+(x, y)`. In fact, the first form is parsed to the second form when it is evaluated. We can confirm it in the REPL: `+(3,4)` returns `7` and `typeof(+)` returns `Function`.

A function can take *a function* (or multiple functions) as its *argument* that calculates the numerical derivative of a function `f`, as defined in the following function:

```
function numerical_derivative(f, x, dx=0.01)

  derivative = (f(x+dx) - f(x-dx))/(2*dx)

  return derivative

end
```

The function can be called as `numerical_derivative(f, 1, 0.001)`, passing an anonymous function `f` as an argument:

```
f = x -> 2x^2 + 30x + 9

println(numerical_derivative(f, 1, 0.001)) #> 33.99999999999537
```

A function can also return another function (or multiple functions) as its *value*. This is demonstrated in the following code that calculates the derivative of a function (which is also a function):

```
function derivative(f)

    return function(x)

  # pick a small value for h

        h = x == 0 ? sqrt(eps(Float64)) : sqrt(eps(Float64)) * x

        xph = x + h

        dx = xph - x

        f1 = f(xph) # evaluate f at x + h

        f0 = f(x) # evaluate f at x

        return (f1 - f0) / dx  # divide by h

    end

end
```

As we can see, both are excellent use cases for anonymous functions.

Here is an example of a `counter` function that returns (a tuple of) two anonymous functions:

```
function counter()
    n = 0
    () -> n += 1, () -> n = 0
end
```

We can assign the returned functions to variables:

```
(addOne, reset) = counter()
```

Notice that n is not defined outside the function:

```
julia> n
ERROR: n not defined
```

Then, when we call `addOne` repeatedly, we get the following code:

```
addOne() #=> 1
addOne() #=> 2
addOne() #=> 3
reset()  #=> 0
```

What we see is that in the `counter` function, the variable n is captured in the anonymous functions. It can only be manipulated by the functions, `addOne` and `reset`. The two functions are said to be **closed** over the variable n and both have references to n. That's why they are called **closures**.

Currying (also called a partial application) is the technique of translating the evaluation of a function that takes multiple arguments (or a tuple of arguments) into evaluating a sequence of functions, each with a single argument. Here is an example of function currying:

```
function add(x)
    return function f(y)
        return x + y
    end
end
```

The output returned is `add (generic function with 1 method)`.

Calling this function with `add(1)(2)` returns 3. This example can be written more succinctly as `add(x) = f(y) = x + y` or with an anonymous function, as `add(x) = y -> x + y`. Currying is especially useful when passing functions around, as we will see in the *Map, filters, and list comprehensions* section.

Recursive functions

Functions can be nested, as demonstrated in the following example:

```
function a(x)
    z = x * 2
    function b(z)
        z += 1
    end
    b(z)
end


d = 5
a(d) #=> 11
```

A function can also be recursive, that is, it can call itself. To show some examples, we need to be able to test a condition in code. The simplest way to do this in Julia is to use the ternary operator ? of the form expr ? b : c (ternary because it takes three arguments). Julia also has a normal if construct (refer to the *Conditional evaluation* section of *Chapter 4, Control Flow*). expr is a condition and if it is true, then b is evaluated and the value is returned, else c is evaluated. This is used in the following recursive definition to calculate the sum of all the integers up to and including a certain number:

```
sum(n) = n > 1 ? sum(n-1) + n : n
```

The recursion ends because there is a base case: when n is 1, this value is returned. Or here is the famous function to calculate the *n*th Fibonacci number that is defined as the sum of the two previous Fibonacci numbers:

```
fib(n) = n < 2 ? n : fib(n-1) + fib(n-2)
```

When using recursion, care should be taken to define a base case to stop the calculation. Also, although Julia can nest very deep, watch out for stack overflow because until now, Julia does not do tail call optimization automatically. If you run into this problem, *Zach Allaun* suggests a nice workaround in the blog at http://blog.zachallaun.com/post/jumping-julia.

Map, filter, and list comprehensions

Maps and filters are typical for functional languages. A **map** is a function of the form map(func, coll), where func is a (often anonymous) function that is successively applied to every element of the coll collection, so map returns a new collection. Some examples are as follows:

- map(x -> x * 10, [1, 2, 3]) returns [10, 20, 30]
- cubes = map(x-> x^3, [1:5]) returns [1, 8, 27, 64, 125]

Map can also be used with functions that take more than one argument. In this case, it requires a collection for each argument, for example, map(*, [1, 2, 3], [4, 5, 6]) works per element and returns [4, 10, 18].

When the function passed to map requires several lines, it can be a bit unwieldy to write this as an anonymous function. For instance, consider using the following function:

```
map( x-> begin
          if x == 0 return 0
          elseif iseven(x) return 2
          elseif isodd(x) return 1
          end
      end, [-3:3])
```

This function returns [1,2,1,0,1,2,1]. This can be simplified with a do block as follows:

```
map([-3:3]) do x
    if x == 0 return 0
    elseif iseven(x) return 2
    elseif isodd(x) return 1
    end
end
```

The do x statement creates an anonymous function with the argument x and passes it as the first argument to map.

A **filter** is a function of the form `filter(func, coll)`, where `func` is a (often anonymous) Boolean function that is checked on each element of the collection `coll`. Filter returns a new collection with only the elements on which `func` is evaluated to true. For example, the following code filters the even numbers and returns `[2, 4, 6, 8, 10]`:

```
filter( n -> iseven(n), [1:10])
```

An incredibly powerful and simple way to create an array is to use a **list comprehension**. This is a kind of an implicit loop that creates the result array and fills it with values. Some examples are as follows:

- `arr = Float64[x^2 for x in 1:4]` creates 4-element `Array{Float64,1}` with elements `1.0`, `4.0`, `9.0`, and `16.0`

- `cubes = [x^3 for x in [1:5]]` returns `[1, 8, 27, 64, 125]`

- `mat1 = [x + y for x in 1:2, y in 1:3]` creates a 2×3 `Array{Int64,2}`:

    2 3 4

    3 4 5

- `table10 = [x * y for x=1:10, y=1:10]` creates a 10×10 `Array{Int64,2}`, and returns the multiplication table of 10

- `arrany = Any[i * 2 for i in 1:5]` creates 5-element `Array{Any,1}` with elements 2, 4, 6, 8, and 10

For more examples, you can refer to the *Dictionaries* section in *Chapter 5, Collection Types*.

Constraining the type as with `arr` is often helpful for the performance. Using typed comprehensions everywhere for explicitness and safety in production code is certainly a best practice.

Generic functions and multiple dispatch

We already saw that functions are inherently defined as generic, that is, they can be used for different types of their arguments. The compiler will generate a separate version of the function each time it is called with arguments of a new type. A concrete version of a function for a specific combination of argument types is called a **method** in Julia. To define a new method for a function (also called **overloading**), just use the same function name but a different signature, that is, with different argument types. A list of all the methods is stored in a virtual method table (`vtable`) on the function itself; methods do not belong to a particular type. When a function is called, Julia will do a lookup in that `vtable` at runtime to find which concrete method it should call based on the types of all its arguments; this is Julia's mechanism of **multiple dispatch**, which neither Python, nor C++ or Fortran implements. It allows open extensions where normal object-oriented code would have forced you to change a class or subclass an existing class and thus change your library. Note that only the positional arguments are taken into account for multiple dispatch, and not the keyword arguments.

For each of these different methods, specialized low-level code is generated, targeted to the processor's instruction set. In contrast to **object-oriented (OO)** languages, `vtable` is stored in the function, and not in the type (or class). In OO languages, a method is called on a single object, `object.method()`, which is generally called **single dispatch**. In Julia, one can say that a function belongs to multiple types, or that a function is specialized or overloaded for different types. Julia's ability to compile code that reads like a high-level dynamic language into machine code that performs like C almost entirely is derived from its ability to do multiple dispatch.

To make this idea more concrete, a function such as `square(x)` = `x * x` actually defines a potentially infinite family of methods, one for each of the possible types of the argument x. For example, `square(2)` will call a specialized method that uses the CPU's native integer multiplication instruction, whereas `square(2.0)` will use the CPU's native floating point multiplication instruction.

Let's see multiple dispatch in action. We will define a function f that takes two arguments n and m returning a string, but in some methods the type of n or m or both is annotated (`Number` is a supertype of `Integer`, refer to the *The type hierarchy – subtypes and supertypes* section in *Chapter 6, More on Types, Methods, and Modules*):

```
f(n, m) = "base case"
f(n::Number, m::Number) = "n and m are both numbers"
f(n::Number, m) = "n is a number"
f(n, m::Number) = "m is a number"
f(n::Integer, m::Integer) = "n and m are both integers"
```

This returns `f (generic function with 5 methods)`.

When n and m have no type as in the base case, then their type is `Any`, the supertype of all types. Let's take a look at how the most appropriate method is chosen in each of the following function calls:

- `f(1.5, 2)` returns `n and m are both numbers`
- `f(1, "bar")` returns `n is a number`
- `f(1, 2)` returns `n and m are both integers`
- `f("foo", [1,2])` returns `base case`

Calling `f(n, m)` will never result in an error, because if no other method matches, the base case will be invoked when we add a new method:

```
f(n::Float64, m::Integer) = "n is a float and m is an integer"
```

The call to `f(1.5,2)` now returns `n is a float and m is an integer`.

To get a quick overview of all the versions of a function, type `methods(fname)` in the REPL. For example, `methods(+)` shows a listing of 149 methods for a generic function +:

```
+(x::Bool) at bool.jl:36
+(x::Bool,y::Bool) at bool.jl:39

...

+(a,b,c) at operators.jl:82
+(a,b,c,xs...) at operators.jl:83
```

You can even take a look in the source code at how they are defined, as in base/`bool.jl` in the local Julia installation or at https://github.com/JuliaLang/julia/blob/master/base/bool.jl, where we can see the addition of bool variables equals to the addition of integers: `+(x::Bool, y::Bool) = int(x) + int(y)`, where `int(false)` is 0 and `int(true)` is 1.

As a second example, `methods(sort)` shows `# 4 methods for generic function "sort"`.

The macro `@which` gives you the exact method that is used and where in the source code that method is defined, for example, `@which 2 * 2` returns `*(x::Int64, y::Int64) at int.jl:47`. This also works the other way around. If you want to know which methods are defined for a certain type, or use that type, ask `methodswith(Type)`. For example, `methodswith(String)` gives the following output:

```
354-element Array{Method,1}:
 write(io::IO,s::String) at string.jl:68
 download(url::String,filename::String) at interactiveutil.jl:322
 …
```

In the source for the `write` method, it is defined as follows:

```
write(io::IO, s::String) = for c in s write(io, c) end
```

As already noted, *type stability* is crucial for the optimal performance. A function is type-stable if the return type(s) of all the output variables can be deduced from the types of the inputs. So try to design your functions with type stability in mind.

Some crude performance measurements (execution time and memory used) on the execution of the functions can be obtained from the macro `@time`, for example:

```
@time fib(35)
```

```
elapsed time: 0.115188593 seconds (6756 bytes allocated)        9227465
```

`@elapsed` only returns the execution time. `@elapsed fib(35)` returns `0.115188593`.

In Julia, the first call of a method invokes the **Low Level Virtual Machine Just In Time (LLVM JIT)** compiler backend (refer to the *How Julia works* section in *Chapter 1, Installing the Julia Platform*), to emit machine code for it, so this *warm-up call* will take a bit longer. Start timing or benchmarking from the second call onwards, after doing a dry run.

When writing a program with Julia, first write an easy version that works. Then, if necessary, improve the performance of that version by profiling it and then fixing performance bottlenecks. We'll come back to the performance measurements in the *Performance tips* section of *Chapter 9, Running External Programs*.

Summary

In this chapter, we saw that functions are the basic building blocks of Julia. We explored the power of functions, their arguments and return values, closures, maps, filters, and comprehensions. However, to make the code in a function more interesting, we need to see how Julia does basic control flow, iterations, and loops. This is the topic of the next chapter.

4
Control Flow

Julia offers many of the control statements that are familiar to the other languages, while also simplifying the syntax for many of them. However, tasks are probably new; they are based on the coroutine concept to make computations more flexible.

We will cover the following topics:

- Conditional evaluation
- Repeated evaluation
- Exception handling
- Scope revisited
- Tasks

Conditional evaluation

Conditional evaluation means that pieces of code are evaluated, depending on whether a Boolean expression is either true or false. The familiar `if-elseif-else-end` syntax is used here, which is as follows:

```
# code in Chapter 4\conditional.jl
var = 7
if var > 10
    println("var has value $var and is bigger than 10.")
elseif var < 10
    println("var has value $var and is smaller than 10.")
else
    println("var has value $var and is 10.")
end
# => prints "var has value 7 and is smaller than 10."
```

The `elseif` (of which, there can be more than one) or `else` branches are optional. The condition in the first branch is evaluated, only the code in that branch is executed when the condition is true and so on; so only one branch ever gets evaluated. No parentheses around condition(s) are needed, but they can be used for clarity. Each expression tested must effectively result in a true or false value, and no other values (such as 0 or 1) are allowed.

Because every expression in Julia returns a value, so also does the `if` expression. We can use this expression to do an assignment depending on a condition. In the preceding case, the return value is nothing since that is what `println` returns.

However, in the following snippet, the value 15 is assigned to z:

```
a = 10
b = 15
z = if a > b  a
    else       b
    end
```

These kind of expressions can be simplified using the ternary operator ? (which we introduced in the *Recursive functions* section in *Chapter 3, Functions*) as follows:

```
z = a > b ? a : b
```

Here, only a or b is evaluated and parentheses ( ) can be added around each clause, as it is necessary for clarity. The ternary operator can be chained, but then it often becomes harder to read. Our first example can be rewritten as follows:

```
var = 7
varout = "var has value $var"
cond = var > 10 ? "and is bigger than 10." : var < 10 ? "and is
    smaller than 10" : "and is 10."
println("$varout $cond") # var has value 7 and is smaller than 10
```

Using short-circuit evaluation (refer to the *Elementary mathematical functions* section in *Chapter 2, Variables, Types, and Operations*), the statements with `if` only are often written as follows:

```
if <cond> <statement> end is written as <cond> && <statement
if !<cond> <statement> end is written as <cond> || <statement>
```

To make this clearer, the first can be read as `<cond>` *and then* `<statement>`, and the second as `<cond>` *or else* `<statement>`.

This feature can come in handy when guarding the parameter values passed into the arguments, which calculates the square root, like in the following function:

```
function sqroot(n::Int)
    n >= 0 || error("n must be non-negative")
    n == 0 && return 0
    sqrt(n)
end
sqroot(4)  #=> 2.0
sqroot(0)  #=> 0.0
sqroot(-6) #=> ERROR: n must be non-negative
```

The `error` statement effectively throws an exception with the given message and stops the code execution (refer to the *Exception handling* section in this chapter).

Julia has no switch/case statement, and the language provides no built-in pattern matching (although one can argue that multiple dispatch is a kind of pattern matching, which is based not on value, but on type). If you need pattern matching, take a look at the `PatternDispatch` and `Match` packages that provide this functionality.

Repeated evaluation

Julia has a `for` loop for iterating over a collection or repeating some code a certain number of times. You can use a `while` loop when the repetition depends on a condition and you can influence the execution of both loops through `break` and `continue`.

The for loop

We already encountered the `for` loop when iterating over the elements e of a collection `coll` (refer to the *Strings* and *Ranges and Arrays* sections in *Chapter 2, Variables, Types, and Operations*). This takes the general form:

```
# code in Chapter 4\repetitions.jl
for e in coll
    # body: process(e) executed for every element e in coll
end
```

Here, coll can be a range, a string, an array, or any other iterable collection (for other uses, also refer to *Chapter 5, Collection Types*). The variable e is not known outside the for loop. When iterating over a numeric range, often = (equal to) is used instead of in:

```
for n = 1:10
    print(x^3)
end
```

(This code can be a one-liner, but is spread over three lines for clarity.) The for loop is generally used when the number of repetitions is known.

Use for i in 1:n rather than for i in [1:n] since the latter allocates an array while the former uses a simpler range object.

If you need to know the index when iterating over the elements of an array, run the following code:

```
arr = [x^2 for x in 1:10]
for i = 1:length(arr)
    println("the $i-th element is $(arr[i])")
end
```

A more elegant way to accomplish this is using the enumerate function as follows:

```
for (ix, val) in enumerate(arr)
    println("the $ix-th element is $val")
end
```

Nested for loops are possible, as in this code snippet, for a multiplication table:

```
for n = 1:5
    for m = 1:5
        println("$n * $m = $(n * m)")
    end
end
```

However, the nested for loops can often be combined into a single outer loop as follows:

```
for n = 1:5, m = 1:5
    println("$n * $m = $(n * m)")
end
```

The while loop

When you want to use looping as long as a condition stays true, use the `while` loop, which is as follows:

```
a = 10; b = 15
while a < b
    # body: process(a)
    println(a)
    a += 1
end
# prints on consecutive lines: 10 11 12 13 14
```

In the body of the loop, something has to change the value of `a` so that the initial condition becomes false and the loop ends. If the initial condition is false at the start, the body of the `while` loop is never executed.

If you need to loop over an array while adding or removing elements from the array, use a `while` loop as follows:

```
arr = [1,2,3,4]
while !isempty(arr)
    print(pop!(arr), ", ")
end
```

The preceding code returns the output as `4, 3, 2, 1`.

The break statement

Sometimes, it is convenient to stop the loop repetition inside the loop when a certain condition is reached. This can be done with the `break` statement, which is as follows:

```
a = 10; b = 150
while a < b
    # process(a)
    println(a)
    a += 1
    if a >= 50
        break
    end
end
```

This prints out the numbers 10 to 49, and then exits the loop when a break is encountered. Here is an idiom that is often used; how to search for a given element in an array, and stop when we have found it:

```
arr = rand(1:10, 10)
println(arr)
# get the index of search in an array arr:
searched = 4
for (ix, curr) in enumerate(arr)
  if curr == searched
    println("The searched element $searched occurs on index $ix")
    break
  end
end
```

A possible output might be as follows:

```
[8,4,3,6,3,5,4,4,6,6]
The searched element 4 occurs on index 2
```

The break statement can be used in the for loops as well as in the while loops. It is, of course, mandatory in a while true ... end loop.

The continue statement

What should you do when you want to skip one (or more) loop repetitions? Then nevertheless, continue with the next loop iteration. For this, you need continue, as in this example:

```
for n in 1:10
  if 3 <= n <= 6
    continue # skip current iteration
  end
  println(n)
end
```

This prints out, 1 2 7 8 9 10, skipping the numbers 3 to 6, using a chained comparison.

There is no repeat-until or do-while construct in Julia. A do-while loop can be simulated as follows:

```
while true
# code
  condition || break
end
```

Exception handling

When executing a program, abnormal conditions can occur, which force the Julia runtime to throw an exception or error, show the exception message and the line where it occurred, and then exit. For example (follow along with the code in `chapter 4\errors.jl`):

- Using the wrong index for an array, for example, `arr = [1,2,3]` and then asking for `arr[0]` causes a program to stop with `ERROR: BoundsError()`

- Calling `sqrt()` on a negative value, for example, `sqrt(-3)` causes `ERROR: DomainError: sqrt will only return a complex result if called with a complex argument, try sqrt(complex(x));` The `sqrt(complex(-3))` function gives the correct result `0.0 + 1.7320508075688772im`

- A syntax error in Julia code will usually result in `LoadError`

Similar to these there are 18 predefined exceptions that Julia can generate (refer to `http://docs.julialang.org/en/latest/manual/control-flow/#man-exception-handling`). They are all derived from a base type, `Exception`.

How can you signal an error condition yourself? You can *call* one of the built-in exceptions by *throwing* such an exception; that is, calling the throw function with the exception as an argument. Suppose an input field, `code`, can only accept the codes listed in `codes = ["AO", "ZD", "SG", "EZ"]`. If code has the value, `AR`, the following test produces `DomainError`:

```
if code in codes
    println("This is an acceptable code")
else
    throw(DomainError())
end
```

A `rethrow()` statement can be useful to hand the current exception to a higher calling code level.

Note that you can't give your own message as an argument to `DomainError()`. This is possible with the `error(message)` function (refer to the *Conditional evaluation* section) with a `String` message. This results in a program to stop with an `ErrorException` function and an `ERROR: message` message.

Some other useful functions that do not cause the program flow to stop and that can help you with testing and debugging are as follows:

- warn("Something is not right here"): This prints or writes to the standard error output (in red in the REPL), WARNING: Something is not right here

- info("Did you know this?"): This prints (in blue in the REPL), INFO: Did you know this?

Creating user-defined exceptions can be done by deriving from the base type, Exception, such as type CustomException <: Exception end (for an explanation of <, refer to the *The type hierarchy – subtypes and supertypes* section in *Chapter 6, More on Types, Methods, and Modules*). These can also be used as arguments to be thrown.

In order to catch and handle the possible exceptions yourself so that the program can continue to run, Julia uses the familiar try-catch-finally construct which includes:

- The **dangerous** code that comes in the try block
- The catch block that stops the exception and allows you to react to the code that threw the exception

Here is an example:

```
    a = []
try
        pop!(a)
catch ex
        println(typeof(ex))
    showerror(STDOUT, ex)
end
```

This example prints the output as follows:

```
ErrorException
    array must be non-empty
```

Popping an empty array generates an exception (as does push!(a,1), but then this is because a is not typed). The variable, ex, contains the exception object, but a plain catch without a variable can also be used. The showerror function is a handy function; its first argument can be any I/O stream, so it could be a file.

To differentiate between the different types of exceptions in the catch block, you can use the following code:

```
try
   # try this code
catch ex
   if isa(ex, DomainError)
      # do this
   elseif isa(ex, BoundsError)
      # do this
   end
end
```

Similar to if and while, try is an expression, so you can assign its return value to a variable. So, run the following code:

```
ret = try
   a = 4 * 2
   catch ex
   end
```

After running the preceding code, ret contains the value 8.

Sometimes, it is useful to have a set of statements to be executed no matter what, for example, to clean up resources. Typical use cases are when reading from a file or a database. We want the file or the database connection to be closed after the execution, regardless of whether an error occurred while the file or database was being processed. This is achieved with the finally clause of a try-catch-finally construct, as in this code snippet:

```
f = open("file1.txt") # returns an IOStream(<file file1.txt>)
try
    # operate on file f
catch ex
finally
    close(f)
end
```

The try-catch-finally full construct guarantees that the finally block is always executed, even when there is a return in try. In general, all the three combinations try-catch, try-finally, and try-catch-finally are possible.

It is important to realize that try-catch should not be used in performance bottlenecks, because the mechanism weighs on performance. Whenever feasible, test a possible exception with normal conditional evaluation.

Scope revisited

The for, while, and try blocks (but not the if blocks) all introduce a new scope. Variables defined in these blocks are only known to that scope. This is called the **local scope**, and nested blocks can introduce several levels of local scope.

Variables with the same name in different scopes can safely be used simultaneously. If a variable exists both in global (that is top level) and local scope, you can distinguish between which one you want to use by prefixing them with the global or local keyword:

- global: This indicates that you want to use the variable from the outer, global scope. This applies to the whole of the current scope block.

- local: This means that you want to define a new variable in the current scope.

The following example will clarify this as follows:

```
# code in Chapter 4\scope.jl
x = 9
function funscope(n)
  x = 0 # x is in the local scope of the function
  for i = 1:n
    local x # x is local to the for loop
    x = i + 1
    if (x == 7)
        println("This is the local x in for: $x") #=> 7
    end
  end
  x
  println("This is the local x in funscope: $x") #=> 0
  global x = 15
end

funscope(10)
println("This is the global x: $x") #=> 15
```

This prints out the following result:

```
This is the local x in for: 7
This is the local x in funscope: 0
This is the global x: 15
```

If the `local` keyword was omitted from the `for` loop, the second `print` statement would print out `11` instead of `7`:

```
This is the local x in for: 7
This is the local x in funscope: 11
This is the global x: 15
```

What is the output when the `global x = 15` statement is left out? In this situation, the program prints out this result:

```
This is the local x in for: 7
This is the local x in funscope: 11
This is the global x: 9
```

 However, needless to say, such name conflicts obscure the code and are a source for bugs, so try to avoid them if possible.

If you need to create a new local binding for a variable, use the `let` block. Execute the following code snippet:

```
anon = cell(2) # returns 2-element Array{Any,1}: #undef  #undef
for i = 1:2
  anon[i] = ()-> println(i)
  i += 1
end
```

Here, both `anon[1]` and `anon[2]` are anonymous functions. When they are called with `anon[1]()` and `anon[2]()`, they print 2 and 3 (the values of `i` when they were created plus one). What if you wanted them to stick to the value of `i` at the moment of their creation? Then, you have to use `let` and change the code to this:

```
anon = cell(2)
for i = 1:2
  let i = i
      anon[i] = ()-> println(i)
  end
  i += 1
end
```

Now, `anon[1]()` and `anon[2]()` print 1 and 2 respectively. Because of `let`, they kept the value of i the same as when they were created.

The `let` statement also introduces a new scope. You can, for example, combine it with `begin` like this:

```
begin
    local x = 1
    let
        local x = 2
        println(x)  #> 2
    end
    x
    println(x)  #> 1
end
```

The `for` loops and comprehensions differ in the way they scope an iteration variable. When i is initialized to 0 before a `for` loop, after executing `for i = 1:10 end`, the variable i is now 10:

```
i = 0
for i = 1:10
end
println(i)   #> 10
```

After executing a comprehension such as `[i for i = 1:10]`, the variable i is still 0:

```
i = 0
[i for i = 1:10 ]
println(i)   #> 0
```

Tasks

Julia has a built-in system for running tasks, which are, in general, known as **coroutines**. With this, a computation that generates values (with a `produce` function) can be suspended as a task, while a consumer task can pick up the values (with a `consume` function). This is similar to the `yield` keyword in Python.

As a concrete example, let's take a look at a `fib_producer` function that calculates the first *n* Fibonacci numbers (refer to the *Recursive functions* section in *Chapter 3, Functions*), but it doesn't return the numbers, it produces them:

```
# code in Chapter 4\tasks.jl
function fib_producer(n)
    a, b = (0, 1)
    for i = 1:n
        produce(b)
        a, b = (b, a + b)
    end
end
```

If you call this function as `fib_producer(5)`, it waits indefinitely. Instead you have to envelop it as a task that takes a function with no arguments:

```
tsk1 = Task( () -> fib_producer(10) )
```

This gives the following output as `Task (runnable) @0x0000000005696180`. The tasks' state is runnable. To get the Fibonacci numbers, start consuming them until `nothing` returns, and the task is finished (state is `done`):

```
consume(tsk1) #=> 1
consume(tsk1) #=> 1
consume(tsk1) #=> 2
consume(tsk1) #=> 3
consume(tsk1) #=> 5
consume(tsk1) #=> 8
consume(tsk1) #=> 13
consume(tsk1) #=> 21
consume(tsk1) #=> 34
consume(tsk1) #=> 55
consume(tsk1) #=> nothing # Task (done) @0x0000000005696180
```

It is as if the `fib_producer` function was able to return multiple times, once for each produce call. Between calls to `fib_producer`, its execution is suspended, and the consumer has control.

The same values can be more easily consumed in a `for` loop, where the loop variable becomes one by one the produced values:

```
for n in tsk1
    println(n)
end
```

This produces 1 1 2 3 5 8 13 21 34 55.

The `Task` constructor argument must be a function with 0 arguments, that's why it is written as an anonymous function, `() -> fib_producer(10)`.

There is a macro `@task` that does the same thing:

```
tsk1 = @task fib_producer(10)
```

The `produce` and `consume` functions use a more primitive function called `yieldto`. Coroutines are not executed in different threads, so they cannot run on separate CPUs. Only one coroutine is running at once, but the language runtime switches between them. An internal scheduler controls a queue of runnable tasks and switches between them based on events, such as waiting for data, or data coming in.

Tasks should be seen as a form of cooperative multitasking in a single thread. Switching between tasks does not consume stack space, unlike normal function calls. In general, tasks have very low overhead; so you can use lots of them if needed. Exception handling in Julia is implemented using `Tasks` as well as servers that accept many incoming connections (refer to the *Working with TCP sockets and servers* section in *Chapter 8, I/O, Networking, and Parallel Computing*).

True parallelism in Julia is discussed in the *Parallel operations and computing* section of *Chapter 8, I/O, Networking, and Parallel Computing*.

Summary

In this chapter, we explored the different control constructs such as `if` and `while`. We also saw how to catch exceptions with `try`/`catch`, and how to throw our own exceptions. Some subtleties of scope were discussed, and finally we got an overview of how to use coroutines in Julia with tasks. Now, we are well equipped to explore more complex types that consist of many elements. This is the topic of the next chapter, *Collection types*.

5
Collection Types

Collection of values appear everywhere in programs, and Julia has the most important built-in collection types. In *Chapter 2, Variables, Types, and Operations*, we introduced two important types of collections: **arrays** and **tuples**. In this chapter, we will look more deeply at multidimensional arrays (or matrices) and in the tuple type as well. A dictionary type, where you can look up a value through a key, is indispensable in a modern language, and Julia has this too. Finally, we will explore the set type. Like arrays, all these types are parameterized; the type of their elements can be specified at object construction time.

Collections are also iterable types, the types over which we can loop with `for` or an iterator producing each element of the collection successively. The iterable types include string, range, array, tuple, dict, and set.

So, the following are the topics for this chapter:

- Matrices
- Tuples
- Dictionaries
- Sets
- An example project: word frequency

Matrices

We know that the notation [1, 2, 3] is used to create an array. In fact, this notation denotes a special type of array, called a (column) **vector** in Julia, as shown in the following screenshot:

To create this as a row vector (1   2   3), use the notation [1 2 3] with spaces instead of commas. This array is of type 1 x 3 Array{Int64,2}, so it has two dimensions. (The spaces used in [1, 2, 3] are for readability only, we could have written this as [1,2,3]).

A matrix is a two- or multi-dimensional array (in fact, a matrix is an alias for the two-dimensional case). In fact, we can write this as follows:

```
Array{Int64, 1} == Vector{Int64} #> true
Array{Int64, 2} == Matrix{Int64} #> true
```

As matrices are so prevalent in data science and numerical programming, Julia has an amazing range of functionalities for them.

To create a matrix, use space-separated values for the columns and semicolon-separated for the rows:

```
// code in Chapter 5\matrices.jl:
matrix = [1 2; 3 4]
    2x2 Array{Int64,2}:
    1   2
    3   4
```

So the column vector from the beginning can also be written as [1; 2; 3]. However, you cannot use commas and semicolons together.

To get the value from a specific element in the matrix, you need to index it by row and then by column, for example, matrix[2, 1] returns the value 3 (row 2, column 1).

Using the same notation, one can calculate products of matrices such as [1 2] * [3 ; 4] is calculated as [1 2] * [3 4], which returns the value 11 (which is equal to 1*3 + 2*4).

To create a matrix from random numbers between 0 and 1, with 3 rows and 5 columns, use ma1 = rand(3, 5), which shows the following results:

```
3x5 Array{Float64,2}:
 0.0626778   0.616528   0.60699    0.709196   0.900165
 0.511043    0.830033   0.671381   0.425688   0.0437949
 0.0863619   0.621321   0.78343    0.908102   0.940307
```

The ndims function can be used to obtain the number of dimensions of a matrix. Consider the following example:

```
julia> ndims(ma1) #> 2
julia> size(ma1) #> a tuple with the dimensions (3, 5)
```

To get the number of rows (3), run the following command:

```
julia>   size(ma1,1) #> 3
```

The number of columns (5) is given by:

```
julia> size(ma1,2) #> 5
julia> length(ma1) #> 15, the number of elements
```

That's why, you will often see this nrows, ncols = size(ma), where ma is a matrix, nrows is the number of rows, and ncols is the number of columns.

If you need an identity matrix, where all the elements are zero, except for the elements on the diagonal that are 1.0, use the eye function with the argument 3 for a 3 x 3 matrix:

```
idm = eye(3)
3x3 Array{Float64,2}:
 1.0   0.0   0.0
 0.0   1.0   0.0
 0.0   0.0   1.0
```

You can easily work with parts of a matrix, known as *slices* that are similar to those used in Python and NumPy as follows:

- `idm[1:end, 2]` or shorter `idm[:, 2]` returns the entire second column
- `idm[2, :]` returns the entire second row
- `idmc = idm[2:end, 2:end]` returns the output as follows:

  ```
  2x2 Array{Float64,2}
      1.0   0.0
      0.0   1.0
  ```

- `idm[2, :] = 0` sets the entire second row to `0`
- `idm[2:end, 2:end] = [ 5 7 ; 9 11 ]` will change the entire matrix as follows:

  ```
      1.0   0.0   0.0
      0.0   5.0   7.0
      0.0   9.0   11.0
  ```

All these slicing operations return copies of the original matrix in Julia v0.3. For instance, a change to `idmc` from the previous example will not change `idm`. To obtain a view of the matrix `idm`, rather than a copy, use the sub function (see `?sub` for details). From v0.4 onwards, slicing will create views into the original array rather than copying the data.

To make an array of arrays (a *jagged* array), use `jarr = fill(Array(Int64,1),3)` and then start initializing every element as an array, for example:

```
jarr[1]=[1,2]
jarr[2]=[1,2,3,4]
jarr[3]=[1,2,3] jarr #=>
3-element Array{Array{Int64,1},1}:
 [1,2]
 [1,2,3,4]
 [1,2,3]
```

If `ma` is a matrix say, `[1 2; 3 4]`, then `ma'` is the transpose matrix `[1 3; 2 4]`:

```
ma:    1  2            ma'   1   3
       3  4                  2   4
```

(`ma'` is an operator notation for the `transpose(ma)` function.)

Multiplication is defined between matrices, as in mathematics, so `ma * ma'` returns the 2 x 2 matrix or type `Array{Int64,2}` as follows:

```
5     11
11    25
```

If you need element-wise multiplication, use `ma .* ma'`, which returns `2 x 2`
`Array{Int64,2}`:

```
1    6
6    16
```

The inverse of a matrix `ma` (if it exists) is given by the `inv(ma)` function. The `inv(ma)`
function returns `2 x 2 Array{Float64,2}`:

```
-2.0    1.0
 1.5   -0.5
```

The inverse means that `ma * inv(ma)` produces the identity matrix:

```
1.0    0.0
0.0    1.0
```

Trying to take the inverse of a singular matrix (a matrix that does not
have a well-defined inverse) will result in `LAPACKException` or
`SingularException`, depending on the matrix type.

Suppose you want to solve the `ma1 * X = ma2` equation, where `ma1`,
`X`, and `ma2` are matrices. The obvious solution is `X = inv(ma1) *`
`ma2`. However, this is actually not that good. It is better to use the built-
in solver, where `X = ma1 \ ma21`. If you have to solve the `X * ma1`
`= ma2` equation, use the solution `X = ma2 / ma1`. The solutions that
use / and \ are much more numerically stable and also much faster.

If `v = [1.,2.,3.]` and `w = [2.,4.,6.]`, and you want to form a 3 x 2 matrix with
these two column vectors, then use `hcat(v, w)` (for horizontal concatenation) to
produce the following output:

```
1.0    2.0
2.0    4.0
3.0    6.0
```

vcat(v,w) (for vertical concatenation) results in a one-dimensional array with all the six elements with the same result as append!(v, w).

Thus, hcat concatenates vectors or matrices along the second dimension (columns), while vcat concatenates along the first dimension (rows). The more general cat can be used to concatenate multi-dimensional arrays along arbitrary dimensions.

There is an even simpler literal notation; to concatenate two matrices a and b with the same number of rows to a matrix c, just execute, c = [a b], now b is appended to the right of a. To put b beneath c, type c = [a; b], which is the same as c = [a, b]. Here is a concrete example, a = [1 2; 3 4] and b = [5 6; 7 8]:

a	B	c = [a b]	c = [a; b]	c = [a, b]
1 2	5 6	1 2 5 6	1 2	1 2
3 4	7 8	3 4 7 8	3 4	3 4
			5 6	5 6
			7 8	7 8

The reshape function changes the dimensions of a matrix to new values if this is possible, for example:

```
reshape(1:12, 3, 4) #> returns a 3x4 array with the values 1 to 12
3x4 Array{Int64,2}:
 1   4   7   10
 2   5   8   11
 3   6   9   12
a = rand(3, 3)   #> produces a 3x3 Array{Float64,2}
3x3 Array{Float64,2}:
 0.332401    0.499608   0.355623
 0.0933291   0.132798   0.967591
 0.722452    0.932347   0.809577
reshape(a, (9,1)) #> produces a 9x1 Array{Float64,2}:
9x1 Array{Float64,2}:
 0.332401
 0.0933291
 0.722452
 0.499608
 0.132798
 0.932347
```

```
0.355623

0.967591

0.809577
```

```
reshape(a, (2,2)) #> does not succeed:
```

```
ERROR: DimensionMismatch("new dimensions (2,2) must be consistent
  with array size 9")
```

When working with arrays that contain arrays, it is important to realize that such an array contains references to the contained arrays, not their values. If you want to make a copy of an array, you can use the `copy()` function, but this produces only a "shallow copy" with references to the contained arrays. In order to make a complete copy of the values, we need to use the `deepcopy()` function.

The following example makes this clear:

```
x = cell(2) #> 2-element Array{Any,1}: #undef #undef
x[1] = ones(2) #> 2-element Array{Float64} 1.0 1.0
x[2] = trues(3) #> 3-element BitArray{1}: true true true
x #> 2-element Array{Any,1}: [1.0,1.0] Bool[true,true,true]
a = x
b = copy(x)
c = deepcopy(x)
# Now if we change x:
x[1] = "Julia"
x[2][1] = false
x #> 2-element Array{Any,1}: "Julia" Bool[false,true,true]
a #> 2-element Array{Any,1}: "Julia" Bool[false,true,true]
is(a, x) #> true, a is identical to x
b #> 2-element Array{Any,1}: [1.0,1.0] Bool[false,true,true]
is(b, x) #> false, b is a shallow copy of x
c #> 2-element Array{Any,1}: [1.0,1.0] Bool[true,true,true]
is(c, x) #> false
```

The value of a remains identical to x when this changes, because it points to the same object in memory. The deep copy c function remains identical to the original x. The b value retains the changes in a contained array of x, but not if one of the contained arrays becomes another array.

As to performance, there is a consensus that using fixed-size arrays can offer a real speed boost. If you know the size, your array `arr` will reach from the start (say 75), then indicate this with `sizehint` to the compiler so that the allocation can be optimized as follows:

```
sizehint(arr, 75) (from v0.4 onwards use sizehint!(arr, 75))
```

To further increase the performance, consider using the statically-sized and immutable vectors and matrices of the package `ImmutableArrays`, which is a lot faster, certainly for small matrices and particularly for vectors.

Tuples

A **tuple** is a fixed-sized group of values separated by commas and optionally surrounded by parentheses ( ). The type of these values can be the same, but it doesn't have to; a tuple can contain values of different types, unlike arrays. A tuple is a heterogeneous container, whereas an array is a homogeneous container. The type of a tuple is just a tuple of the types of the values it contains. So, in this sense, a tuple is very much the counterpart of an array in Julia. Also, changing a value in a tuple is not allowed; tuples are immutable.

In *Chapter 2, Variables, Types, and Operations*, we saw fast assignment, which is made possible by tuples:

```
// code in Chapter 5\tuples.jl:
a, b, c, d = 1, 22.0, "World", 'x'
```

This expression assigns a value 1, b becomes 22.0, c takes up the value World, and d becomes x.

The expression returns a tuple (1, 22.0, "World", 'x'), as the REPL shows as follows:

```
julia> a, b, c, d = 1, 22.0, "World", 'x'
(1,22.0,"World",'x')
```

If we assign this tuple to a variable t1 and ask for its type, we get the following result:

```
typeof(t1) #> (Int64,Float64,ASCIIString,Char)
```

The argument list of a function (refer to the *Defining functions* section in *Chapter 3, Functions*) is, in fact, also a tuple. Similarly, Julia simulates the possibility of returning multiple values by packaging them into a single tuple, and a tuple also appears when using functions with variable argument lists. ( ) represents the empty tuple, and (1,) is a one-element tuple. The type of a tuple can be specified explicitly through a type annotation (refer to the *Types* section in *Chapter 2, Variables, Types, and Operations*), such as ('z', 3.14)::(Char, Float64).

The following snippet shows that we can index tuples in the same way as arrays: brackets, indexing starting from 1, slicing, and index control:

```
t3 = (5, 6, 7, 8)
t3[1] #> 5
t3[end] #> 8
t3[2:3] #> (6, 7)
t3[5] #> BoundsError
t3[3] = 9 #> Error: 'setindex' has no matching ...
author = ("Ivo", "Balbaert", 59)
author[2] #> "Balbaert"
```

To iterate over the elements of a tuple, use a `for` loop:

```
for i in t3
    println(i)
end # #> 5  6  7  8
```

A tuple can be *unpacked* or deconstructed like this: `a, b = t3`; now a is 5 and b is 6. Notice that we don't get an error despite the left-hand side not being able to take all the values of `t3`. To do this, we would have to write `a, b, c, d = t3`.

In the following example, the elements of the `author` tuple are unpacked into separate variables: `first_name, last_name,` and `age = author`.

So, tuples are nice and simple types, which make a lot of things possible. We'll find them back in the next section as elements of a dictionary.

Dictionaries

When you want to store and look up the values based on a unique key, then the Dictionary type `Dict` (also called hash, associative collection, or map in other languages) is what you need. It is basically a collection of two-element tuples of the form `(key, value)`. To define a dictionary `d1` as a literal value, the following syntax is used:

```
// code in Chapter 5\dicts.jl:
d1 = [1 => 4.2, 2 => 5.3]
```

It returns `Dict{Int64,Float64}` with 2 entries: `2 => 5.3`   `1 => 4.2`, so there are two key-value tuples here, `(1, 4.2)` and `(2, 5.3)`; the key appears before the `=>` symbol and the value appears after it, and the tuples are separated by commas. The `[ ]` indicates a typed dictionary; all the keys must have the same type, and the same is true for the values. A dynamic version of a dictionary can be defined with `{ }`:

- `d1 = {1 => 4.2, 2 => 5.3}` is `Dict{Any,Any}`

- `d2 = {"a" => 1, (2,3) => true}` is `Dict{Any,Any}`

`Any` is also inferred when a common type among the keys or values cannot be detected. In general, dictionaries that have type `{Any, Any}` tend to lead to lower performance since the JIT compiler does not know the exact type of the elements. Dictionaries used in performance-critical parts of the code should therefore be explicitly typed. Notice that the (key, value) pairs are not returned (or stored) in the key order. If the keys are of type `Char` or `String`, you can also use `Symbol` as the key type, which could be more appropriate since `Symbols` are immutable. For example, `d3 = [:A => 100, :B => 200]`, which is `Dict{Symbol,Int64}`.

Use the bracket notation with a key as an index to get the corresponding value, `d3[:B]` returns `200`. However, the key must exist, else we will get an error, `d3[:Z]` that returns `ERROR: key not found: :Z`. To get around this, use the `get` method and provide a default value that is returned instead of the error, `get(d3, :Z, 999)` returns `999`.

Here is a dictionary that resembles an object, storing the field names as symbols in the keys:

```
dmus = [ :first_name => "Louis", :surname => "Armstrong",
    :occupation => "musician", :date_of_birth => "4/8/1901" ]
```

To test if a (key, value) tuple is present, you can use `in` as follows:

- `in((:Z, 999), d3)` or `(:Z, 999) in d3` returns false

- `in((:A, 100), d3)` or `(:A, 100) in d3` returns true

Dictionaries are *mutable*: if we tell Julia to execute `d3[:A] = 150`, then the value for key `:A` in `d3` has changed to `150`. If we do this with a new key, then that tuple is added to the dictionary:

```
d3[:C] = 300
```

`d3` is now `[:A => 150, :B => 200, :C => 300]`, and it has three elements: `length(d3)` returns `3`.

d4 = Dict() is an empty dictionary of type Any, and start populating it in the same way as in the example with d3.

d5 = Dict{Float64, Int64}() is an empty dictionary with key type Float64 and value type Int64. As to be expected, adding keys or values of another type to a typed dictionary is an error. d5["c"] = 6 returns ERROR: 'convert' has no method matching   convert(::Type{Float64}, ::ASCIIString) and d3["CVO"] = 500 returns ERROR: CVO is not a valid key for type Symbol.

Deleting a key mapping from a collection is also straightforward. delete!(d3, :B) removes (:B, 200) from the dictionary, and returns the collection that contains only :A => 100.

Keys and values – looping

To isolate the keys of a dictionary, use the keys function ki = keys(d3), with ki being a KeyIterator object, which we can use in a for loop as follows:

```
for k in keys(d3)
    println(k)
end
```

This prints out A and B. This gives us also an easier way to test if a key exists with in, for example, :A in keys(d3) returns true and :Z in keys(d3) returns false.

An equivalent method is haskey(d3, :A), which also returns true. If you want to work with an array of the keys, use collect(keys(d3)) that returns a two-element Array{Symbol,1} that contains :A and :B. To obtain the values, use the values function: vi = values(d3), with vi being a ValueIterator object, which we can also loop through with for:

```
for v in values(d3)
    println(v)
end
```

This returns 100 and 200, but the order in which the values or keys are returned is undefined.

Creating a dictionary from arrays with keys and values is trivial because we have a Dict constructor that can use these. For example:

```
keys1 = ["J.S. Bach", "Woody Allen", "Barack Obama"] and
values1 =  [ 1685, 1935, 1961]
```

Then, d5 = Dict(keys1, values1) results in a Dict{ASCIIString, Int64} with three entries as follows:

```
d5 = [ "J.S. Bach" => 1685, "Woody Allen" => 1935,
  "Barack Obama" => 1961 ]
```

Working with both the key and value pairs in a loop is also easy. For instance, the following for loop over d5 is as follows:

```
for (k, v) in d5
        println("$k was born in $v")
    end
```

This will print the following output:

```
J.S. Bach was born in 1685
Barack Obama was born in 1961
Woody Allen was born in 1935
```

Or alternatively, using an index in every (key,value) tuple of d5:

```
for p in d5
  println("$(p[1]) was born in $(p[2])")
end
```

If the key-value pairs are arranged in a single array, like this:

```
dpairs = ["a", 1, "b", 2, "c", 3]
```

Then, you can build a dictionary from this array with the following comprehension:

```
d6 = [dpairs[i] => dpairs[i+1] for i in 1:2:length(dpairs)]
```

Here, 1:2:length(dpairs) iterates over the array in steps of two: i will therefore take on values 1, 3, and 5.

If you want it typed, prefix it with (String => Int64) like this:

```
d6 = (String => Int64)[dpairs[i] => dpairs[i+1] for i in
  1:2:length(dpairs)]
```

Here is a nice example of the use of a dictionary with the built-in function `factor`. The function `factor` takes an integer and returns a dictionary with the prime factors as the keys, and the number of times each prime appears in the product as values:

```
function showfactor(n)
  d = factor(n)
    println("factors for $n")
    for (k, v) in d
        print("$k^$v\t")
    end
end
```

`@time showfactor(3752)` outputs the following result:

```
factors for 3752
7^1     2^3     67^1    elapsed time: 0.000458578 seconds
    (2472 bytes allocated)
```

Here are some more neat tricks, where `dict` is a dictionary:

- Copying the keys of a dictionary to an array with a list comprehension:
  ```
  arrkey = [key for (key, value) in dict]
  ```
  This is the same as `collect(keys(dict))`.

- Copying the values of a dictionary to an array with a list comprehension:
  ```
  arrval = [value for (key, value) in dict]
  ```
  This is the same as `collect(values(dict))`

- Make an array with the first *n* values of a dictionary when the keys are the integers from *1* to *n* and beyond:
  ```
  arrn = [dict[i] for i = 1:n]
  ```

  This can also be written as a map, `arrn = map((i) -> dict[i], [1:n])`

From Julia v0.4 onwards, the following literal syntaxes or the `Dict` constructors are deprecated:

```
d1 = [1 => 4.2, 2 => 5.3]
d2 = {"a"=>1, (2,3)=>true}
capitals = (String => String)["France"=> "Paris",
  "China"=>"Beijing"]
d5 = Dict(keys1, values1)
```

They take the new forms as follows:

```
d1 = Dict(1 => 4.2, 2 => 5.3)
d2 = Dict{Any,Any}("a"=>1, (2,3)=>true)
capitals = Dict{String, String}("France"=> "Paris",
  "China"=>"Beijing") # from v0.4 onwards
d5 = Dict(zip(keys1, values1))
```

This is indicated for all the examples in the accompanying code file, dicts.jl. It can be difficult to make packages to work on both the versions. The Compat package (https://github.com/JuliaLang/Compat.jl) was created to help with this, as it provides compatibility constructs that will work in both the versions without warnings.

Sets

Array elements are ordered, but can contain duplicates, that is, the same value can occur at different indices. In a dictionary, keys have to be unique, but the values do not, and the keys are not ordered. If you want a collection where *order does not matter*, but where the *elements* have to be *unique*, then use a **Set**. Creating a set is easy as this:

```
// code in Chapter 5\sets.jl:
s = Set({11, 14, 13, 7, 14, 11})
```

The Set() function creates an empty set. The preceding line returns Set{Int64} ({7,14,13,11}), where the duplicates have been eliminated. From v0.4 onwards, the {} notation with sets is deprecated; you should use s = Set(Any[11, 14, 13, 7, 14, 11]). In the accompanying code file, the latest version is used.

The operations from the set theory are also defined for s1 = Set({11, 25}) and s2 = Set({25, 3.14}) as follows:

- union(s1, s2) produces Set{Any}({3.14,25,11})
- intersect(s1, s2) produces Set{Any}({25})
- setdiff(s1, s2) produces Set{Any}({11}), whereas setdiff(s2, s1) produces Set{Any}({ 3.14})
- issubset(s1, s2) produces false, but issubset(s1, Set({11, 25, 36})) produces true

To add an element to a set is easy: push!(s1, 32) adds 32 to set s1. Adding an existing element will not change the set. To test, if a set contains an element, use in. For example, in(32, s1) returns true and in(100, s1) returns false.

Be careful if you want to define a set of arrays: `Set([1,2,3])` produces a set of integers `Set{Int64}({2,3,1})`; to get a set of arrays, use `Set({[1,2,3]})` that returns `Set{Any}({[1,2,3]})`.

Sets are commonly used when we need to keep a track of objects in no particular order. For instance, we might be searching through a graph. We can then use a set to remember which nodes of the graph we already visited in order to avoid visiting them again. Checking whether an element is present in a set is independent of the size of the set. This is extremely useful for very large sets of data. For example:

```
x = Set([1:100])
@time 2 in x  # elapsed time 4.888e-6 seconds
x2 = Set([1:1000000])
@time 2 in x2 # elapsed time 5.378e-6 seconds
```

Both the tests take approximately the same time, despite the fact that x2 is four orders of magnitude larger than x.

Making a set of tuples

You can start by making an empty set as this: `st = Set{(Int, Int)}()`.

Then, you can use `push!` to start filling it up: `push!(st, (1,2))`, which returns a `Set{(Int64,Int64)}({(1,2)})`, and so on. Another possibility is to use `[ ]`, for example, `st2 = Set({(1, 2), (5, 6)})` produces a set with the two tuples `(1,2)` and `(5,6)`.

Let's take a look at the `Collections` module if you need more specialized containers. It contains a priority queue as well as some lower level heap functions.

Example project – word frequency

A lot of the concepts and techniques that we have seen so far in the book come together in this little project. Its aim is to read a text file, remove all the characters that are not used in words, and count the frequencies of the words in the remaining text. This can be useful, for example, when counting the word density on a web page, the frequency of DNA sequences, or the number of hits on a website that came from various IP addresses. This can be done in some 10 lines of code. For example, when `words1.txt` contains the sentence `to be, or not to be, that is the question!`, then this is the output of the program:

```
Word : frequency

be : 2
is : 1
not : 1
or : 1
question : 1
that : 1
the : 1
to : 2
```

Here is the code with comments:

```
# code in chapter 5\word_frequency.jl:
# 1- read in text file:
str = readall("words1.txt")
# 2- replace non alphabet characters from text with a space:
nonalpha = r"(\W\s?)" # define a regular expression
str = replace(str, nonalpha, ' ')
digits = r"(\d+)"
str = replace(str, digits, ' ')
# 3- split text in words:
word_list = split(str, ' ')
# 4- make a dictionary with the words and count their frequencies:
word_freq = Dict{String, Int64}()
for word in word_list
    word = strip(word)
    if isempty(word) continue end
    haskey(word_freq, word) ?
      word_freq[word] += 1 :
      word_freq[word] = 1
end
# 5- sort the words (the keys) and print out the frequencies:
println("Word : frequency \n")
words = sort!(collect(keys(word_freq)))
for word in words
    println("$word : $(word_freq[word])")
end
```

The `isempty` function is quite general and can be used on any collection.

Try the code out with the example text files `words1.txt` or `words2.txt`. See the output in `results_words1.txt` and `results_words2.txt`.

Summary

In this chapter, we looked at the built-in collection types Julia has to offer. We saw the power of matrices, the elegance of dictionaries, and the usefulness of tuples and sets. However, to dig deeper into the fabric of Julia, we need to learn how to define new types, another concept necessary to organize the code. We must know how types can be constructed, and how they are used in multiple dispatch. This is the main topic of the next chapter, where we will also see modules, which serve to organize code, but at an even higher level than types.

6
More on Types, Methods, and Modules

Julia has a rich built-in type system, and most data types can be *parameterized*, such as `Array{Float64, 2}` or `Dict{Symbol, Float64}`. **Typing** a variable (or more exactly the value it is bound to) is *optional*, but indicating the type of some variables, although it is not statically checked, can gain some of the advantages of static type systems as in C++, Java, or C#. A Julia program can run without any indication of types, which can be useful in a prototyping stage, and it will still run fast. However, some type indications can increase the performance by allowing more specialized multiple dispatch. Moreover, typing function parameters makes the code easier to read and understand. The robustness of the program is also enhanced by throwing exceptions in cases where certain type operations are not allowed. These failures will manifest during testing, or the code can provide an exception handling mechanism.

All functions in Julia are inherently *generic* or *polymorphic*, that is, they can operate on different types of their arguments. The most appropriate method (an implementation of the function where argument types are indicated) will be chosen at runtime to be executed, depending on the type of arguments passed to the function. As we will see in this chapter, you can also define your own types, and Julia provides a limited form of abstract types and subtyping.

A lot of these topics have already been discussed in the previous chapters; for example, refer to the *Generic functions and multiple dispatch* section in *Chapter 3, Functions*. In this chapter, we broaden the previous discussions by covering the following topics:

- Type annotations and conversions
- The type hierarchy – subtypes and supertypes
- Concrete and abstract types
- User-defined and composite types
- Type unions
- Parametric types
- Parametric and constructor methods
- Standard modules and paths

Type annotations and conversions

As we saw previously, type annotating a variable is done with the `::` operator, such as in the function definition, `function write(io::IO, s::String) #… end`, where the parameter `io` has to be of type `IO`, and `s` of type `String`. To put it differently, `io` has to be an instance of type `IO`, and `s` an instance of type `String`. The `::` operator is, in fact, an assertion that affirms that the value on the left is of the type on the right. If this is not true, a `typeassert` error is thrown. Try this out in the REPL:

```
# see the code in Chapter 6\conversions.jl:
(31+42)::Float64
```

We get an `ERROR: type: typeassert: expected Float64, got Int64` error message.

This is in addition to the method specialization for multiple dispatch, an important reason why type annotations are used in function signatures.

The operator `::` can also be used in the sense of a type declaration, but only in local scope such as in functions, as follows:

```
n::Int16 or local n::Int16 or n::Int16 = 5
```

Every value assigned to `n` will be implicitly converted to the indicated type with the `convert` function.

Type conversions and promotions

The `convert` function can also be used explicitly in the code as `convert(Int64, 7.0)`, which returns `7`.

In general, `convert(Type, x)` will attempt to put the `x` value in an instance of `Type`. In most cases, `type(x)` will also do the trick, as in `int64(7.0)`.

The conversion, however, doesn't always work:

- When precision is lost: `convert(Int64, 7.01)` returns an `ERROR: InexactError()` error message, however, `int64(7.01)` rounds off and converts to the nearest integer, producing the output as `7`

- When the target type is incompatible with the source value: `convert(Int64, "CV")` returns an `ERROR: `convert` has no method matching convert(::Type{Int64}, ::ASCIIString)` error message

This last error message really shows us how multiple dispatch works; the types of the input arguments are matched against the methods available for that function.

We can define our own conversions by providing new methods for the `convert` function. For example, for information on how to do this, refer to `http://docs.julialang.org/en/latest/manual/conversion-and-promotion/#conversion`.

Julia has a built-in system called **automatic type promotion** to promote arguments of mathematical operators and assignments to a common type: in `4 + 3.14`, the integer `4` is promoted to a `Float64` value, so that the addition can take place that results in `7.140000000000001`. In general, promotion refers to the conversion of values of different types to one common type. This can be done with the `promote` function, which takes a number of arguments, and returns a tuple of the same values, converting them to a common type. An exception is thrown if promotion is not possible. Some examples are as follows:

- `promote(1, 2.5, 3//4)` returns `(1.0, 2.5, 0.75)`
- `promote(1.5, im)` returns `(1.5 + 0.0im, 0.0 + 1.0im)`
- `promote(true, 'c', 1.0)` returns `(1.0, 99.0, 1.0)`

Thanks to the automatic type promotion system for numbers, Julia doesn't have to define, for example, the + operator for any combinations of numeric types. Instead, it is defined as `+(x::Number, y::Number) = +(promote(x,y)...)`.

It basically says that first, promote the arguments to a common type, and then perform the addition. A number is a common supertype for all values of numeric types. To determine the common promotion type of the two types, use `promote_type(Int8, Uint16)` to find whether it returns `Int64`.

This is because somewhere in the standard library the following `promote_rule` function was defined as `promote_rule(::Type{Int8}, ::Type{Uint16}) = Int64`.

You can take a look at how promoting is defined in the source code of Julia in `base/promotion.jl`. These kinds of promotion rules can be defined for your own types too if needed.

The type hierarchy – subtypes and supertypes

(Follow along with the code in `Chapter 6\type_hierarchy.jl`.)

In Julia, every value has a type, for example, `typeof(2)` is `Int64` (or `Int32` on 32-bit systems). Julia has a lot of built-in types, in fact, a whole hierarchy starting from the type `Any` at the top. Every type in this structure also has a type, namely, `DataType`, so it is very consistent: `typeof(Any)`, `typeof(Int64)`, `typeof(Complex{Int64})`, and `typeof(DataType)` all return `DataType`. So, types in Julia are also objects; all concrete types, except tuple types, which are a tuple of the types of its arguments, are of type `DataType`.

This type hierarchy is like a tree; each type has one parent given by the `super` function:

- `super(Int64)` **returns** `Signed`
- `super(Signed)` **returns** `Integer`
- `super(Integer)` **returns** `Real`
- `super(Real)` **returns** `Number`
- `super(Number)` **returns** `Any`
- `super(Any)` **returns** `Any`

A type can have a lot of children or `subtypes` as follows:

- `subtypes(Integer)` form `5-element Array{Any,1}` that contains `BigInt`, `Bool`, `Char`, `Signed`, and `Unsigned`

- `subtypes(Signed)` form `5-element Array{Any,1}` that contain `Int128`, `Int16`, `Int32`, `Int64`, and `Int8`

- `subtypes(Int64)` is `0-element Array{Any,1}`, and it has no subtypes

To indicate the subtype relationship, the operator `<` is used: `Bool <: Integer` and `Bool <: Any` return true, while `Bool <: Char` is false. An equivalent form uses the `issubtype` function: `issubtype(Bool, Integer)` is true, but `issubtype(Float64, Integer)` returns false.

Here is a visualization of part of this type tree:

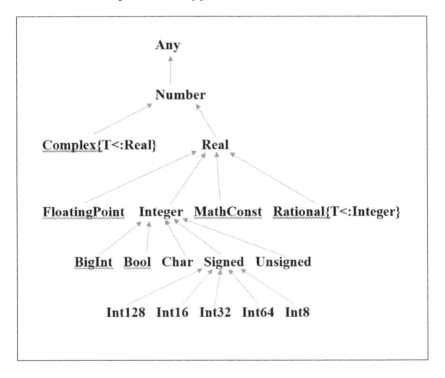

Concrete and abstract types

In this hierarchy, some types, such as Number, Integer, and Signed, are abstract, which means that they have no concrete objects or values of their own. Instead, objects or values are of concrete types given by the result of applying typeof(value), such as Int8, Float64, and UTF8String. For example, the concrete type of the value 5 is Int64 given by typeof(5) (on a 64-bit machine). However, a value has also the type of all of its supertypes, for example, isa(5, Number) returns true (we introduced the isa function in the *Types* section of *Chapter 2, Variables, Types, and Operations*).

Concrete types have no subtypes and might only have abstract types as their supertypes. Schematically, we can differentiate them as follows:

Type	Instantiate	Subtypes
concrete	Y	N
abstract	N	Y

An abstract type (such as Number and Real) is only a name that groups multiple subtypes together, but it can be used as a type annotation or used as a type in array literals. These types are the nodes in the type hierarchy that mainly serve to support the type tree. Also, note that an abstract type cannot have any fields.

Julia's type tree can be graphically visualized by running the following command:

```
julia julia_types.jl > tree.txt
```

Here is a little fragment of its output:

```
. . . +- Integer << abstract immutable size:0 >>
. . . . +- Signed << abstract immutable size:0 >>
. . . . . +- FileOffset = Int64 << concrete immutable
pointerfree size:8 >>
. . . . . +- Cssize_t = Int64 << concrete immutable
pointerfree size:8 >>
. . . . . +- Clonglong = Int64 << concrete immutable
pointerfree size:8 >>
. . . . . +- Cchar = Int8 << concrete immutable pointerfree
size:1 >>
. . . . . +- Clong = Int32 << concrete immutable pointerfree
size:4 >>
. . . . . +- Cint = Int32 << concrete immutable pointerfree
size:4 >>
. . . . . +- Int8 << concrete immutable pointerfree
size:1 >>
. . . . . . +- Integer64 =
Union(Uint16,Uint8,Int8,Uint32,Int16,Int64,Int32,Uint64)
. . . . . . +- SmallSigned = Union(Int8,Int16,Int32)
. . . . . . +- Signed64 = Union(Int8,Int16,Int64,Int32)
. . . . . +- Int16 << concrete immutable pointerfree
size:2 >>
. . . . . . +- Integer64 =
Union(Uint16,Uint8,Int8,Uint32,Int16,Int64,Int32,Uint64)
. . . . . . +- SmallSigned = Union(Int8,Int16,Int32)
. . . . . . +- Signed64 = Union(Int8,Int16,Int64,Int32)
. . . . . +- Coff_t = Int64 << concrete immutable
pointerfree size:8 >>
. . . . . +- Int128 << concrete immutable pointerfree
size:16 >>
. . . . . . +- CommonReduceResult =
Union(Float32,Int128,Float64,Int64,Uint128,Uint64)
. . . . . +- Cptrdiff_t = Int64 << concrete immutable
pointerfree size:8 >>
. . . . . +- Int64 << concrete immutable pointerfree
size:8 >>
. . . . . . +- Integer64 =
Union(Uint16,Uint8,Int8,Uint32,Int16,Int64,Int32,Uint64)
```

The abstract type Any is the supertype of all types, and all the objects are also instances of Any.

At the other end is None; all types are supertypes of None and no object is an instance of None. The None type has no values and no subtypes, it is unlikely that you will ever have to use this type.

Different from None is the type Nothing; this has one value named nothing. When a function is only used for its side effects, convention dictates that it returns nothing. We have seen this with the println function, where the printing is the side effect, for instance:

```
x = println("hello") #> hello
x == nothing #> true
```

From v0.4 onwards, these types are named differently: None becomes Union(), and Nothing becomes Void.

User-defined and composite types

In Julia, as a developer, you can define your own types to structure data used in applications. For example, if you need to represent points in a three-dimensional space, you can define a type Point as follows:

```
# see the code in Chapter 6\user_defined.jl:
type Point
    x::Float64
    y::Float64
    z::Float64
end
```

The type Point is a concrete type, objects of this type can be created as p1 = Point(2, 4, 1.3), and it has no subtypes: typeof(p1) returns Point (constructor with 2 methods), subtypes(Point) returns 0-element Array{Any,1}.

Such a *user-defined* type is composed of a set of named fields with an optional type annotation; that's why it is a *composite* type, and its type is also DataType. If the type of a named field is not given, then it is Any. A composite type is similar to a struct in C or a class without methods in Java.

Unlike in other object-oriented languages such as Python or Java, where you call a function on an object such as object.func(args), Julia uses the func(object, args) syntax.

Julia has no classes (as types with functions belong to that type); this keeps the data and functions separate. Functions and methods for a type will be defined outside that type. Methods cannot be tied to a single type, because multiple dispatch connects them with different types. This provides more flexibility, because when adding a new method for a type, you don't have to change the code of the type itself, as you would have to do with the code of the class in object-oriented languages.

The names of the fields that belong to a composite type can be obtained with the `names` function of the type or an object: `names(Point)` or `names(p1)` returns `3-element Array{Symbol,1}: :x :y :z`.

A user-defined type has two default implicit *constructors* that have the same name as the type and take an argument for each field. You can see this by asking for the methods of `Point`: `methods(Point)` returns `2 methods for generic function "Point": Point(x::Float64, y::Float64, z::Float64)` and `Point(x ,y ,z)`. Here, the field values can be of type `Any`.

You can now make objects simply like this:

```
orig = Point(0, 0, 0)
p1 = Point(2, 4, 1.3).
```

Fields that together contain the state of the object can be accessed by the name as in: `p1.y` that returns `4.0`.

Objects of such a type are *mutable*, for example, I can change the `z` field to a new value with `p1.z = 3.14`, resulting in `p1` now having the value `Point(2.0, 4.0, 3.14)`. Of course, types are checked: `p1.z = "A"` results in an error.

Objects as arguments to functions are *passed by reference*, so that they can be changed inside the function (for example, refer to the function `insert_elem(arr)` in the *Defining types* section of *Chapter 3, Functions*).

If you don't want your objects to be changeable, replace `type` with the keyword `immutable`, for example:

```
immutable Vector3D
    x::Float64
    y::Float64
    z::Float64
end
```

Calling `p = Vector3D(1, 2, 3)` returns `Vector3D(1.0, 2.0, 3.0)` and `p.y = 5` returns `ERROR: type Vector3D is immutable`.

Immutable types enhance the performance, because Julia can optimize the code for them. Another big advantage of immutable types is thread safety: an immutable object can be shared between threads without needing synchronization.

If, however, such an immutable type contains a mutable field such as an array, the contents of that field can be changed. So, define your immutable types without mutable fields.

A type once defined cannot be changed. If we try to define a new type `Point` with fields of type `Int64`, or with added fields, we get an `ERROR: invalid redefinition of constant TypeName` error message.

A new type that is exactly the same as an existing type can be defined as an *alias*, for instance, `typealias Point3D Point`. Now, objects of type `Point3D` can also be created: `p31 = Point3D(1, 2, 3)` that returns `Point(1.0, 2.0, 3.0)`. Julia also uses this internally; the alias `Int` is used for either `Int64` or `Int32`, depending on the architecture of the system that is being used.

When are two values or objects equal or identical?

To check whether two values are equal or not can be decided by the `==` operator, for example, `5 == 5` and `5 == 5.0` are both `true`. To see whether the two objects x and y are identical, they must be compared with the `is` function, and the result is a Boolean value, `true` or `false`:

```
is(x, y) -> Bool
```

The `is(x, y)` function can also be written with the three `=` signs as `x === y`.

Objects such as numbers are immutable and they are compared at the bits level: `is(5, 5)` returns `true` and `is(5, 5.0)` returns `false`.

For objects that are more complex, such as strings, arrays, or objects that are constructed from composite types, the addresses in memory are compared to check whether they point to the same memory location. For example, if `q = Vector3D(4.0, 3.14, 2.71)`, and `r = Vector3D(4.0, 3.14, 2.71)`, then `is(q, r)` returns `false`.

Multiple dispatch example

Let's now explore an example about people working in a company to show multiple dispatch in action. Let's define an abstract type `Employee` and a type `Developer` that is a subtype:

```
abstract Employee
type Developer <: Employee
    name::String
    iq
    favorite_lang::String
end
```

We cannot make objects from an abstract type: calling `Employee()` only returns an `ERROR: type cannot be constructed` error message.

The type `Developer` has two implicit constructors, but we can define another *outer constructor* that uses a default constructor as follows:

```
Developer(name, iq) = Developer(name, iq, "Java")
```

Outer constructors provide additional convenient methods to construct objects. Now, we can make the following two developer objects:

- `dev1 = Developer("Bob", 110)` that returns `Developer("Bob",110,"Java")`
- `dev2 = Developer("William", 145, "Julia")` that returns `Developer("William",145,"Julia")`

Similarly, we can define a type `Manager` and an instance of it as follows:

```
type Manager
    name::String
    iq
    department::String
end
man1 = Manager("Julia", 120, "ICT")
```

Concrete types, such as `Developer` or `Manager`, cannot be subtyped:

```
type MobileDeveloper <: Developer
platform
end
```

This returns `ERROR: invalid subtyping in definition of MobileDeveloper`.

If we now define a function `cleverness` as `cleverness(emp::Employee) = emp.iq`, then `cleverness(devel1)` returns `110`, but `cleverness(man1)` returns an `ERROR: `cleverness` has no method matching cleverness(::Manager)` error message; the function has no method for a manager.

Suppose we introduce a function `cleverer` with the following argument types:

```
function cleverer(d::Developer, e::Employee)
    println("The developer $(d.name) is cleverer I think!")
end
```

The `cleverer(devel1, devel2)` function will now print `"The developer Bob is cleverer I think!"` (Clearly, the function isn't yet coded right, we are biased in thinking that developers are always more intelligent). It matches a method because `devel2` is also an employee. However, `cleverer(devel1, man1)` will give an `ERROR: `cleverer` has no method matching cleverer(::Developer, ::Manager)` error message, as a manager is not an employee, and a method with this signature was not defined.

We now define another method for `cleverer` as follows:

```
function cleverer(e::Employee, d::Developer)
    if e.iq <= d.iq
        println("The developer $(d.name) is cleverer!")
    else
        println("The employee $(e.name) is cleverer!")
    end
end
```

Now an ambiguity arises; Julia detects a problem in the definitions and gives us the following warning:

```
Warning: New definition
    cleverer(Employee,Developer) at none:2
is ambiguous with:
    cleverer(Developer,Employee) at none:2.
To fix, define
    cleverer(Developer,Developer)
before the new definition.
```

The ambiguity is that if `cleverer` is called with `e` being a `Developer`, which of the two defined methods should be chosen? Julia takes a pragmatic standpoint and `cleverer(devel1, devel2)` still gives the same outcome. However, now we will define the more specific (and correct) method as follows:

```
function cleverer(d1::Developer, d2::Developer)
    if d1.iq <= d2.iq
        println("The developer $(d2.name) is cleverer!")
    else
        println("The developer $(d1.name) is cleverer!")
    end
end
```

Now, `cleverer(devel1, devel2)` prints `"The developer William is cleverer!"` as well as `cleverer(devel2, devel1)`. This illustrates multiple dispatching. When defined, the more specific method definition (here, the second method `cleverer`) is chosen. More specific means the method with more specialized type annotations for its arguments. More specialized doesn't only mean subtypes, it can also mean using type aliases.

 Always avoid method ambiguities by specifying an appropriate method for the intersection case.

Types and collections – inner constructors

Here is another type with only default constructors:

```
# see the code in Chapter 6\inner_constructors.jl
type Person
    firstname::String
    lastname::String
    sex::Char
    age::Float64
    children::Array{String, 1}
end
p1 = Person("Alan", "Bates", 'M', 45.5, ["Jeff", "Stephan"])
```

This example demonstrates that an object can contain collections such as arrays or dictionaries. Custom types can also be stored in a collection, just like built-in types, for example:

```
people = Person[]
```

This returns `0-element Array{Person,1}`.

```
push!(people, p1)
push!(people, Person("Julia", "Smith", 'F', 27, ["Viral"]))
```

The `show(people)` function now returns the following output:

```
[Person("Alan","Bates",'M',45.5,String["Jeff","Stephan"]),
 Person("Julia","Smith",'F',27.0,String["Viral"])]
```

Now, we can define a function `fullname` on type `Person`. You notice that the definition stays outside the type's code:

```
fullname(p::Person) = "$(p.firstname) $(p.lastname)"
```

Or, slightly more performant:

```
fullname(p::Person) = string(p.firstname, " ", p.lastname)
```

Now, `print(fullname(p1))` returns `Alan Bates`.

If you need to include error checking or transformations as part of the type construction process, you can use inner constructors (so-called because they are defined inside the type itself), as shown in the following example:

```
type Family
    name::String
    members::Array{String, 1}
    big::Bool
  Family(name::String) = new(name, String[], false)
  Family(name::String, members) = new(name, members,
    length(members) > 4)
end
```

We can make a `Family` object as follows:

```
fam = Family("Bates-Smith", ["Alan", "Julia", "Jeff", "Stephan",
  "Viral"])
```

Then the output is as follows:

```
Family("Bates-Smith",String["Alan","Julia","Jeff","Stephan","Viral"],tr
ue)
```

The keyword `new` can only be used in an inner constructor to create an object of the enclosing type. The first constructor takes one argument and generates a default for the other two values. The second constructor takes two arguments and infers the value of `big`. Inner constructors give you more control over how values of the type can be created. Here, they are written with the short function notation, but if they are multiline, they would use the normal function syntax.

Note that when you use inner constructors, there are no default constructors anymore. Outer constructors calling a limited set of inner constructors is often the best practice.

Type unions

In geometry, a two-dimensional point and a vector are not the same, even if they both have an *x* and *y* component. In Julia, we can also define them as different types as follows:

```
    # see the code in Chapter 6\unions.jl
type Point
    x::Float64
    y::Float64
end

type Vector2D
    x::Float64
    y::Float64
end
```

Here are the two objects:

- `p = Point(2, 5)` that returns `Point(2.0, 5.0)`
- `v = Vector2D(3, 2)` that returns `Vector2D(3.0, 2.0)`

Suppose we want to define the sum for these types as a point that has coordinates as the sum of the corresponding coordinates:

```
+(p, v)
```

This results in an ERROR: `+` has no method matching +(::Point, ::Vector2D) error message.

Even after defining the following, + (p, v) still returns the same error because of multiple dispatch (Julia has no way of knowing that + (p, v) should be the same as + (v, p)):

```
+(p::Point,    q::Point) = Point(p.x + q.x, p.y + q.y)
+(u::Vector2D, v::Vector2D) = Point(u.x + v.x, u.y + v.y)
+(u::Vector2D, p::Point) = Point(u.x + p.x, u.y + p.y)
```

Only when we define the type matching method as + (p::Point, v::Vector2D) = Point(p.x + v.x, p.y + v.y), we get a result + (p, v) that returns Point(5.0,7.0).

Now, you can ask the question: doesn't multiple dispatch and many types give rise to code duplication as in the case here?

However, this is not so because in such a case, we can define a union type VecOrPoint:

```
VecOrPoint = Union(Vector2D, Point)
```

If p is a point, it is also of type VecOrPoint, and the same is true for a Vector2D v: isa(p, VecOrPoint) and isa(v, VecOrPoint) both return true.

Now, we can define one + method that works for any of the preceding four cases:

```
+(u::VecOrPoint, v:: VecOrPoint) = VecOrPoint(u.x + v.x, u.y +
  v.y)
```

So, now we only need one method instead of four.

Parametric types and methods

An array can take elements of different types, so, we can have, for example, arrays of the following types: Array{Int64,1}, Array{Int8,1}, Array{Float64,1}, or Array{ASCIIString, 1}, and so on. That is why an Array is a **parametric type**; its elements can be of any arbitrary type T, written as Array{T, 1}.

In general, types can take **type parameters**, so that type declarations actually introduce a whole family of new types. Returning to the Point example of the previous section, we can generalize it to the following:

```
# see the code in Chapter 6\parametric.jl
type Point{T}
  x::T
  y::T
end
```

(This is conceptually similar to generic types in Java or templates in C++).

This abstract type creates a whole family of new possible concrete types (but they are only compiled as needed at runtime), such as `Point{Int64}`, `Point{Float64}`, and `Point{String}`.

These are all subtypes of `Point`: `issubtype(Point{String}, Point)` that return `true`. However, this is not the case when comparing different `Point` types, whose parameter types are subtypes of one another: `issubtype(Point{Float64}, Point{Real})` returns `false`.

To construct objects, you can indicate the type `T` in the constructor, as in `p = Point{Int64}(2, 5)`, but this can be shortened to `p = Point(2, 5)`, or let's consider another example: `p = Point("London", "Great-Britain")`.

If you want to restrict the parameter type `T` to only the subtypes of `Real`, this can be written as follows:

```
type Point{T <: Real}
  x::T
  y::T
end
```

Now, the statement `p = Point("London", "Great-Britain")` results in an `ERROR:` `` `Point{T<:Real}` `` `has no method matching Point{T<:Real}(::ASCIIString, : ASCIIString)` error message, because `String` is not a subtype of `Real`.

Much in the same way, methods also optionally can have type parameters immediately after their name and before the tuple of arguments, for example, to constrain two arguments to be of the same type `T`, run the following command:

```
add{T}(x::T, y::T) = x + y
```

Now, `add(2, 3)` returns 5 and `add(2, 3.0)` returns an ERROR: `` `add` `` has no method matching `add(::Int64, ::Float64)` error message.

Here, we restrict `T` to be a subtype of `Number` in `add` as follows:

```
add{T <: Number}(x::T, y::T) = x + y
```

As another example, here is how to check whether a `vecfloat` function only takes a vector of floating point numbers as the input. Simply, define it with a type parameter `T` as follows:

```
function vecfloat{T <: FloatingPoint}(x::Vector{T})
# code
end
```

Inner constructors can also take type parameters in their definition.

Standard modules and paths

The code of Julia packages (also called **libraries**) is contained in a module, whose name starts with an uppercase letter by convention like this:

```
# see the code in Chapter 6\modules.jl
module Package1
# code
end
```

This serves to separate all its definitions from those in the other modules, so that no name conflicts occur. Name conflicts are solved by qualifying the function by the module name. For example, the packages `Winston` and `Gadfly` both contain a function plot. If needed these two versions in the same script, we would write this as follows:

```
import Winston
import Gadfly
Winston.plot(rand(4))
Gadfly.plot(x=[1:10], y=rand(10))
```

All variables defined in the `global` scope are automatically added to the `Main` module. Thus, when you write `x = 2` in the REPL, you are adding the variable `x` to the `Main` module.

Julia starts with `Main` as the current top-level module. The module `Core` contains all built-in identifiers, and it is always available. The standard library is also available. All of its code (the contents of `/base`) is contained in the modules `Base`, `Pkg`, `Collections`, `Graphics`, `Test`, and `Profile`.

The type of a module is `Module: typeof(Base)` that returns `Module`. If we call `names(Main)`, we get, for example, 6-element `Array{Symbol,1}:` `:ans`, `:a`, `:vecfloat`, `:Main`, `:Core`, `:Base`, depending on what you have defined in the REPL.

All the top-level defined variables and functions, together with the default modules are stored as symbols. The `whos()` function lists these objects with their types:

```
Base                    Module
Core                    Module
Main                    Module
a                        Int64
ans                      6-element Array{Symbol,1}
vecfloat                Function
```

This can also be used for another module, for example, `whos(Winston)` lists all the exported names from the module `Winston`.

A module can make some of its internal definitions such as constants, variables, types, functions, and so on visible to other modules (make them `public`) by declaring them with `export`, for example:

```
export Type1, perc
```

If a module `LibA` (among others) is defined in a `modules_ext.jl` file, then the statement `require("modules_ext.jl")` will load this in the current code. Using `LibA`, will make all its exported names available in the current namespace; this is what we did in the REPL to load a package.

For the preceding example, using `Package1` will make the type `Type1` and function `perc` available in other modules that import them through this statement. All the other definitions remain invisible (or `private`).

Here is a more concrete example. Suppose we define a `TemperatureConverter` module as follows:

```
#code in Chapter 6\temperature_converter.jl
module TemperatureConverter

  export as_celsius

  function as_celsius(temperature, unit)
    if unit == :Celsius
      return temperature
    elseif unit == :Kelvin
```

```
        return kelvin_to_celsius(temperature)
    end
  end

  function kelvin_to_celsius(temperature)
    # 'private' function
    return temperature + 273
  end

end
```

We can now use this module in another program as follows:

```
#code in Chapter 6\using_module.jl
require("temperature_converter.jl")

using TemperatureConverter

println("$(as_celsius(100, :Celsius))") #> 100
println("$(as_celsius(100, :Kelvin))") #> 373
# println("$(kelvin_to_celsius(0))") #> ERROR: kelvin_to_celsius
  not defined
```

The function kelvin_to_celsius was not exported, and so is not known in the program using_module.jl.

In general, there are different ways of importing definitions from another module LibA in the current module:

- First, make use of using LibA, then LibA will be searched for exported definitions if needed. A function from LibA can then be used without qualifying it with the module name.

- If you want to be more selective, you can execute using LibB.varB or the shorthand, using LibC: varC, funcC.

- The import LibD.funcD statement only imports one name and can also be used if funcD was not exported; the function funcD must be used as LibD.funcD.

- Use importall LibE to import all the exported names in LibE.

Imported variables are read-only, and the current module cannot create variables with the same names as the imported ones. A source file can contain many modules, or one module can be defined in several source files. If a module contains a function __init__(), this will be executed when the module is first loaded.

As we saw in *Chapter 1*, *Installing the Julia Platform*, a module can also include other source files in their entirety with `include("file1.jl")`, but then, the included files are not modules. Using `include("file1.jl")` is, to the compiler, no different to copying `file1.jl` and pasting it directly in the current file or the REPL.

The variable `LOAD_PATH` contains a list of directories where Julia looks for (module) files when running the `using`, `import`, or `include` statements. It can be set up at the operating system level: in a start-up script such as `.bashrc` or `.profile`, or in `Environment Variables` on Windows. You can extend this variable in the code using `push!`:

```
push!(LOAD_PATH, "new/path/to/search")
```

Modules are compiled on load, which slows down Julia's start-up time in the current version. This will improve considerably once precompiling of modules is possible, which is planned for Version 0.4.

Summary

In this chapter, we delved into types and type hierarchy in Julia. We got a much better understanding of types and how functions work on them through multiple dispatch. The next chapter will reveal another power tool in Julia: **metaprogramming and macros**.

7
Metaprogramming in Julia

Everything in Julia is an expression that returns a value when executed. Every piece of the program code is internally represented as an ordinary Julia data structure, also called an **expression**. In this chapter, we will see that by working on expressions, how a Julia program can transform and even generate the new code, which is a very powerful characteristic, also called **homoiconicity**. It inherits this property from **Lisp**, where code and data are just lists, and where it is commonly referred to with the phrase: "**code is data and data is code**". We will explore this metaprogramming power by covering the following topics:

- Expressions and symbols
- Eval and interpolation
- Defining macros
- Built-in macros
- Reflection capabilities

Expressions and symbols

An **abstract syntax tree** (**AST**) is a tree representation of the abstract syntactic structure of the source code written in a programming language. When Julia code is parsed by its LLVM JIT compiler, it is internally represented as an abstract syntax tree. The nodes of this tree are simple data structures of type expression Expr.

(For more information on abstract syntax trees, refer to http://en.wikipedia.org/wiki/Abstract_syntax_tree).

An expression is simply an object that represents Julia code. For example, `2 + 3` is a piece of code, which is an expression of type `Int64` (follow along with the code in `Chapter 7\expressions.jl`). Its syntax tree can be visualized as follows:

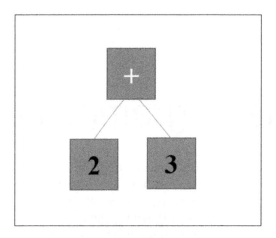

To make Julia see this as an expression and block its evaluation, we have to quote it, that is, precede it by a colon (`:`) as in `:(2 + 3)`. When you evaluate `:(2 + 3)` in the REPL, it just returns `:(2 + 3)`, which is of type `Expr`: `typeof(:(2 + 3))` returns `Expr`. In fact, the `:` operator (also called the **quote** operator) means to treat its argument as data, not as code.

If this code is more than one line, enclose them between the `quote` and `end` keywords to turn the code into an expression, for example, this expression just returns itself:

```
quote
    a = 42
    b = a^2
    a - b
end
```

In fact, this is the same as `:(a = 42; b = a^2; a - b)`. `quote ... end` is just another way to convert blocks of code into expressions.

We can give such an expression a name, such as `e1 = :(2 + 3)`. We can then inquire if `e1` has fields with `names(e1)`, which returns `3-element Array{Symbol,1}`: `:head, :args, :typ`.

These return the following information:

- `e1.head` returns `:call`, indicating the kind of expression, which here is a function call

- `e1.args` returns 3-element `Array{Any,1}`:   `:+`   `2`   `3`

- `e1.typ` returns `Any`; it is used by the type inference mechanism to store type annotations

Indeed the expression `2 + 3` is, in fact, a call of the + function with the argument `2` and `3`: `2 + 3 == + (2, 3)` returns `true`. The `args` argument consists of a symbol `:+` and two literal values `2` and `3`. Expressions are made of symbols and literals. More complicated expressions will consist of literal values, symbols, and sub- or nested expressions, which can, in turn, be reduced to symbols and literals.

For example, consider the expression `e2 = :(2 + a * b - c)`, which can be visualized by the following syntax tree:

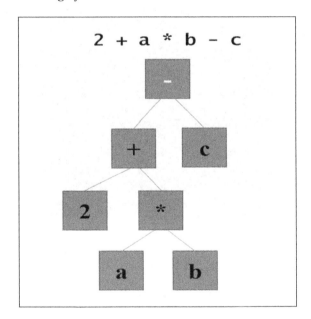

`e2` consists of `e2.args`, which is a 3-element `Array{Any,1}` that contains `:-` and `:c`, which are symbols, and `:(2 + a * b)`, which is also an expression. This last expression, in turn, is itself an expression with `args :+, 2,` and `:(a * b)`; `:(a * b)` is an expression with arguments and symbols: `:*, :a,` and `:b`. We can see that this works recursively; we can simplify every subexpression in the same way until we end up with elementary symbols and literals.

In the context of an expression, *symbols are used to indicate access to variables;* they represent the variable in the tree structure of the code. In fact, the **"prevent evaluation"** character of the `quote` operator (`:`) is already at work with the symbols: after x = 5 , x returns 5 , but :x returns :x.

With this knowledge, we can conclude that the definition of the type `Expr` in Julia goes as follows:

```
type Expr
   head::Symbol
   args::Array{Any,1}
   typ
end
```

The `dump` function presents the abstract syntax tree for its argument in a nice way. For example, `dump(:(2 + a * b - c))` returns the output, as shown in the following screenshot:

```
julia> dump(:(2 + a * b - c))
Expr
  head: Symbol call
  args: Array(Any,(3,))
    1: Symbol -
    2: Expr
      head: Symbol call
      args: Array(Any,(3,))
        1: Symbol +
        2: Int64 2
        3: Expr
          head: Symbol call
          args: Array(Any,(3,))
          typ: Any
      typ: Any
    3: Symbol c
  typ: Any
```

Eval and interpolation

With the definition of type `Expr` from the preceding section, we can also build expressions directly from the constructor for `Expr`, for example: e1 = Expr(:call, *, 3, 4) returns :((*) (3, 4)) (follow along with the code in `Chapter 7\eval.jl`).

The result of an expression can be computed with the `eval` function, eval(e1), which returns 12 in this case. At the time an expression is constructed, not all the symbols have to be defined, but they have to be at the time of evaluation, otherwise an error occurs.

For example, e2 = Expr(:call, *, 3, :a) returns :((*)(3, a)) and eval(e2) then, gives ERROR: a not defined. Only after we say, for example, a = 4 does eval(e2) and returns 12.

Expressions can also change the state of the execution environment, for example, the expression e3 = :(b = 1) assigns a value to b when evaluated, and even defines b if it doesn't exist already.

To make writing expressions a bit simpler, we can use the $ operator to do **interpolation** in expressions; as with $ in strings, and this will evaluate immediately when the expression is made. The expressions a = 4 and b = 1, e4 = :(a + b) return :(a + b) and e5 = :($a + b) returns :(4 + b); both the expressions evaluate to 5. So, there are two kinds of evaluations here:

- Expression interpolation (with $) evaluates when the expression is constructed (at parse time)
- Quotation (with : or quote) evaluates only when the expression is passed to eval at runtime

We now have the capability to build the code programmatically; inside a Julia program, we can construct the arbitrary code while it is running, and then evaluate this with eval. So, Julia can generate the code from inside itself during the normal program execution.

This happens all the time in Julia and it is used, for example, to do things such as to generate bindings for external libraries, to reduce the repetitive boilerplate code needed to bind big libraries, or to generate lots of similar routines in other situations. Also, in the field of robotics, the ability to generate another program and then, run it is very useful. For example: a chirurgical robot learns how to move by perceiving a human surgeon demonstrate a procedure. Then, the robot generates the program code from that perception, so that it is able to perform the procedure by itself.

One of the most powerful Julia tools emerging from what we discussed until now is **macros**, which exist in all the languages of the Lisp family.

Defining macros

In the previous chapters, we already used macros, such as @printf in *Chapter 2*, *Variables, Types, and Operations*, and @time in *Chapter 3*, *Functions*. Macros are like functions, but instead of values, they take expressions (which can also be symbols or literals) as input arguments. When a macro is evaluated, the input expression is expanded, that is, the macro returns a modified expression. This expansion occurs at parse time when the syntax tree is being built, not when the code is actually executed.

The following highlights the difference between macros and functions when they are called or invoked:

- **Function**: It takes the input values and returns the computed values at runtime
- **Macro**: It takes the input expressions and returns the modified expressions at parse time

In other words, a macro is a custom program transformation. Macros are defined with the keyword as follows:

```
macro mname
# code returning expression
end
```

It is invoked as `@mname exp1 exp2` or `@mname(exp1, exp2)` (the `@` sign distinguishes it from a normal function call). The macro block defines a new scope. Macros allow us to control when the code is executed.

Here are some examples:

- A first simple example is a `macint` macro, which does the interpolation of its argument expression `ex`:

```
# see the code in Chapter 7\macros.jl)
macro macint(ex)
    quote
        println("start")
        $ex
        println("after")
    end
end
```

`@macint println("Where am I?")` will result in:

```
start

Where am I?

after
```

- The second example is an `assert` macro that takes an expression `ex` and tests whether it is true or not, in the last case, an error is thrown:

```
macro assert(ex)
:($ex ? nothing : error("Assertion failed: ",
    $(string(ex))))
end
```

For example: `@assert 1 == 1.0` returns nothing. `@assert 1 == 42` returns `ERROR: Assertion failed: 1 == 42`.

The macro replaces the expression with a ternary operator expression, which is evaluated at runtime. To examine the resulting expression, use the `macroexpand` function as follows:

```
macroexpand(:(@assert 1 == 42))
```

This returns the following expression:

```
:(if 1 == 42
        nothing
    else
        error("Assertion failed: ", "1 == 42")
    end)
```

This `assert` function is just a macro example, use the built-in assert function in the production code (refer to the *Testing* subsection of the *Built-in macro's* section).

* The third example mimics an `unless` construct, where branch is executed if the condition `test` is not true:

```
macro unless(test, branch)
    quote
        if !$test
            $branch
        end
    end
end
```

Suppose `arr = [3.14, 42, 'b']`, then `@unless 42 in arr println("arr does not contain 42")` returns nothing, but `@unless 41 in arr println("arr does not contain 41")` prints out the following command:

```
arr does not contain 41
```

Here, `macroexpand(:(@unless 41 in arr println("arr does not contain 41")))` returns the following output:

```
quote  # none, line 3:
    if !(41 in arr) # line 4:
        println("arr does not contain 41")
    end
end
```

- The fourth example shows how to convert an array of strings to an array of type T with a convarr macro.

  Suppose the array is arr = ["a", "b", "c"], then, we define a macro as follows:

  ```
  macro convarr(arr, T)
      :(reshape($T[$arr...], size($arr)...))
  end
  ```

  Notice how the destination type T is general. The reshape function is used here to redimension the array (this is its signature: Base.reshape(arr, dims)) so, this macro will work for arrays of arbitrary dimensions.

  For example, calling @convarr arr Symbol returns 3-element Array{Symbol,1} :a :b :c.

Unlike functions, macros inject the code directly in the namespace in which they are called, possibly this is also in a different module than in which they were defined. It is therefore important to ensure that this generated code does not clash with the code in the module in which the macro is called. When a macro behaves appropriately like this, it is called a **hygienic macro**. The following rules are used when writing hygienic macros:

- Declare the variables used in the macro as local, so as not to conflict with the outer variables

- Use the escape function esc to make sure that an interpolated expression is not expanded, but instead is used literally

- Don't call eval inside a macro (because it is likely that the variables you are evaluating don't even exist at that point)

These principles are applied in the following timeit macro that times the execution of an expression ex (like the built-in macro @time):

```
macro timeit(ex)
    quote
        local t0 = time()
        local val = $(esc(ex))
        local t1 = time()
        print("elapsed time in seconds: ")
        @printf "%.3f" t1 - t0
        val
    end
end
```

The expression is executed through `$`, and `t0` and `t1` are respectively the start and end times.

`@timeit factorial(10)` **returns** `elapsed time in seconds: 0.0003628800.`

`@timeit a^3` **returns** `elapsed time in seconds: 0.0013796416.`

Hygiene with macros is all about differentiating between the macro context and the calling context.

Macros are valuable tools to save you a lot of tedious work and with the quoting and interpolation mechanism, they are fairly easy to create. You will see them being used everywhere in Julia for lots of different tasks. Ultimately, they allow you to create domain-specific languages (DSLs). To get a better idea of this concept, we suggest you experiment with the other examples in the accompanying code file.

Built-in macros

Needless to say the Julia team has put macros to good use. To get the help information about a macro, enter a `?` in the REPL, and type `@macroname` after the `help>` prompt, or type `help("@macroname")`. Apart from the built-in macros we encountered in the examples in the previous chapters, here are some other very useful ones (refer to the code in `Chapter 7\built_in_macros.jl`).

Testing

The `@assert` macro actually exists in the standard library. The standard version also allows you to give your own error message, which is printed after `ERROR: assertion failed`.

The `Base.Test` library contains some useful macros to compare the numbers:

```
using Base.Test
@test 1 == 3
```

This returns `ERROR: test failed: 1 == 3`.

`@test_approx_eq` tests whether the two numbers are approximately equal. `@test_approx_eq 1 1.1` returns `ERROR: assertion failed: |1 - 1.1| <= 2.220446049250313e-12` because they are not equal within the machine tolerance. However, you can give the interval as the last argument within which they should be equal to `@test_approx_eq_eps 1 1.1 0.2`, which returns nothing, so `1` and `1.1` are within `0.2` from each other.

Debugging

If you want to look up in the source code where and how a particular method is defined, use `@which`, for example: if `arr = [1, 2]` then `@which sort(arr)` returns `sort(v::AbstractArray{T,1}) at sort.jl:334`.

`@show` shows the expression and its result, which is handy for checking the embedded results: `456 * 789 + (@show 2 + 3)` gives `2 + 3 => 5      359789`.

Benchmarking

For benchmarking purposes, we already know `@time` and `@elapsed`; `@timed` gives you the `@time` results as a tuple:

`@time [x^2 for x in 1:1000]` prints `elapsed time: 3.911e-6 seconds (8064 bytes allocated)` and returns `1000-element Array{Int64,1}: ....`

`@timed [x^2 for x in 1:1000]` returns `([1, 4, 9, 16, 25, 36, 49, 64, 81, 100  …  982081, 984064, 986049, 988036, 990025, 992016, 994009, 996004, 998001, 1000000], 3.911e-6, 8064, 0.0)`.

`@elapsed [x^2 for x in 1:1000]` returns `3.422e-6`.

If you are specifically interested in the allocated memory, use `@allocated [x^2 for x in 1:1000]` which returns `8064`.

To time code execution, call `tic()` to start timing, execute the function, and then use `toc()` or `toq()` to end the timer:

```
tic()
[x^2 for x in 1:1000]
```

The `toc()` function prints `elapsed time: 0.024395069 seconds`.

Starting a task

Tasks (refer to the *Tasks* section in *Chapter 4*, *Control Flow*) are independent units of code execution. Often, we want to start executing them, and then continue executing the main code without waiting for the task result. In other words, we want to start the task *asynchronously*. This can be done with the `@async` macro:

```
a = @async 1 + 2 # Task (done) @0x000000002d70faf0
consume(a) # 3
```

For a list of the built-in macros we encountered in this book, consult the list of macros in *Appendix*, *List of Macros and Packages*.

Reflection capabilities

We saw in this chapter that the code in Julia is represented by expressions that are data structures of type `Expr`. The structure of a program and its types can therefore be explored programmatically just like any other data. This means that a running program can dynamically discover its own properties, which is called **reflection**. We already have encountered many of these functions before:

* `typeof` and `subtypes` to query the type `hierarchy` (refer to *Chapter 6, More on Types, Methods, and Modules*)

* `methods(f)` to see all the methods of a function `f` (refer to *Chapter 3, Functions*)

* `names` and `types`: given a type `Person`:

```
type Person
    name:: String
    height::Float64
end
```

Then, `names(Person)` returns the field names as symbols: `2-element Array{Symbol,1}: :name    :height`.

`Person.types` returns a tuple with the field types `(String, Float64)`.

* To inspect how a function is represented internally, you can use `code_lowered`:

```
code_lowered(+, (Int, Int))
```

This returns the following output:

```
1-element Array{Any,1}:
:($(Expr(:lambda, {:x,:y}, {{},{{:x,:Any,0},{:y,:Any,0}},{}},
    :(begin  # int.jl
, line 33:
        return box(Int64,add_int(unbox(Int64,x),unbox(Int64,y)))
    end))))
```

Or, you can use `code_typed` to see the type-inferred form:

```
code_typed(+, (Int, Int))
```

This returns the following:

```
1-element Array{Any,1}:
 :($(Expr(:lambda, {:x,:y}, {{},{{:x,Int64,0},{:y,Int64,0}},{}},
:(begin  # int.
```

```
jl, line 33:
        return box(Int64,add_int(x::Int64,y::Int64))::Int64
    end::Int64))))
```

> Using `code_typed` can show you whether your code is type optimized for performance: if the Any type is used instead of an appropriate specific type you would expect, then type indication in your code can certainly be improved, leading most likely to speed up the program's execution.

- To inspect the code generated by the LLVM engine, use `code_llvm`, and to see the assembly code generated, use `code_native` (refer to the *How Julia works* section in *Chapter 1, Installing the Julia Platform*).

While reflection is not necessary for many of the programs that you will write, it is very useful for IDEs to be able to inspect the internals of an object as well as for the tools generating the automatic documentation and for profiling tools. In other words, reflection is indispensable for tools that need to inspect the internals of the code objects programmatically.

Summary

In this chapter, we explored the expression format in which Julia is parsed. Because this format is a data structure, we can manipulate this in the code, and this is precisely what macros can do. We explored a number of them, and also some of the built-in ones that can be useful. In the next chapter, we will extend our vision to the network environment in which Julia runs, and we will explore its powerful capabilities for parallel execution.

8
I/O, Networking, and Parallel Computing

In this chapter, we will explore how Julia interacts with the outside world, reading from standard input and writing to standard output, files, networks, and databases. Julia provides asynchronous networking I/O using the `libuv` library. We will see how to handle data in Julia. We will also discover the parallel processing model of Julia.

In this chapter, the following topics are covered:

- Basic input and output
- Working with files (including the CSV files)
- Using DataFrames
- Working with TCP sockets and servers
- Interacting with databases
- Parallel operations and computing

Basic input and output

Julia's vision on input/output (I/O) is **stream-oriented**, that is, reading or writing streams of bytes. We will introduce different types of streams, such as file streams, in this chapter. **Standard input (stdin)** and **standard output (stdout)** are constants of the type TTY (an abbreviation for the old term, Teletype) that can be used in the Julia code to read from and write to (refer to the code in Chapter 8\io.jl):

- `read(STDIN, Char)`: This command waits for a character to be entered, and then returns that character; for example, when you type in J, this returns **'J'**

- `write(STDOUT, "Julia")`: This command types out **Julia5** (the added **5** is the number of bytes in the output stream; it is not added if the command ends in a semicolon (;))

  `STDIN` and `STDOUT` are simply streams and can be replaced by any stream object in the read/write commands. `readbytes` is used to read a number of bytes from a stream into a vector:

- `readbytes(STDIN,3)`: This command waits for an input, for example, `abe` reads 3 bytes from it, and then returns `3-element Array{Uint8,1}: 0x61 0x62 0x65`

- `readline(STDIN)`: This command reads all the inputs until a newline character \n is entered, for example, type `Julia` and press *ENTER*, this returns **"Julia\r\n"** on Windows and **"Julia\n"** on Linux

If you need to read all the lines from an input stream, use the `eachline` method in a `for` loop, for example:

```
stream = STDIN
for line in eachline(stream)
    print("Found $line")
    # process the line
end
```

For example:

```
First line of input
Found First line of input
2nd line of input
Found 2nd line of input
3rd line...
Found 3rd line...
```

To test whether you have reached the end of an input stream, use `eof(stream)` in combination with a `while` loop as follows:

```
while !eof(stream)
    x = read(stream, Char)
    println("Found: $x")
# process the character
end
```

We can experiment with replacing stream by `STDIN` in these examples.

Working with files

To work with files, we need the `IOStream` type. `IOStream` is a type with the supertype `IO` and has the following characteristics:

- The fields are given by `names(IOStream)`

  `4-element Array{Symbol,1}:` `:handle` `:ios` `:name` `:mark`

- The types are given by `IOStream.types`

  `(Ptr{None}, Array{Uint8,1}, String, Int64)`

The file handle is a pointer of the type `Ptr`, which is a reference to the file object.

Opening and reading a line-oriented file with the name `example.dat` is very easy:

```
// code in Chapter 8\io.jl
fname = "example.dat"
f1 = open(fname)
```

`fname` is a string that contains the path to the file, using escaping of special characters with \ when necessary; for example, in Windows, when the file is in the `test` folder on the `D:` drive, this would become `d:\\test\\example.dat`. The `f1` variable is now an `IOStream(<file example.dat>)` object.

To read all lines one after the other in an array, use `data = readlines(f1)`, which returns `3-element Array{Union(ASCIIString,UTF8String),1}`:

```
"this is line 1.\r\n"
"this is line 2.\r\n"
"this is line 3."
```

For processing line by line, now only a simple loop is needed:

```
for line in data
  println(line) # or process line
end
close(f1)
```

Always close the `IOStream` object to clean and save resources. If you want to read the file into one string, use `readall` (for example, see the program `word_frequency` in *Chapter 5, Collection Types*). Use this only for relatively small files because of the memory consumption; this can also be a potential problem when using `readlines`.

There is a convenient shorthand with the do syntax for opening a file, applying a function process, and closing it automatically. This goes as follows (file is the IOStream object in this code):

```
open(fname) do file
    process(file)
end
```

As you can recall, in the *Map, filter, and list comprehensions* section in *Chapter 3, Functions*, do creates an anonymous function, and passes it to open. Thus, the previous code example would have been equivalent to open(process, fname). Use the same syntax for processing a file fname line by line without the memory overhead of the previous methods, for example:

```
open(fname) do file
    for line in eachline(file)
        print(line) # or process line
    end
end
```

Writing a file requires first opening it with a "w" flag, then writing strings to it with write, print, or println, and then closing the file handle that flushes the IOStream object to the disk:

```
fname =    "example2.dat"
f2 = open(fname, "w")
write(f2, "I write myself to a file\n")
# returns 24 (bytes written)
println(f2, "even with println!")
close(f2)
```

Opening a file with the "w" option will clear the file if it exists. To append to an existing file, use "a".

To process all the files in the current folder (or a given folder as an argument to readdir()), use this for loop:

```
for file in readdir()
  # process file
end
```

Reading and writing CSV files

A CSV file is a comma-separated file. The data fields in each line are separated by commas ", " or another delimiter such as semicolons "; ". These files are the de-facto standard for exchanging small and medium amounts of tabular data. Such files are structured so that one line contains data about one *data object*, so we need a way to read and process the file line by line. As an example, we will use the data file `Chapter 8\winequality.csv` that contains 1,599 sample measurements, 12 data columns, such as `pH` and `alcohol` per sample, separated by a semicolon. In the following screenshot, you can see the top 20 rows:

	fixed acidi	volatile ac	citric acid	residual su	chlorides	free sulfur	total sulfu	density	pH	sulphates	alcohol	quality
2	7.4	0.7		0	1.9	0.076	11	34	0.9978	3.51	0.56	9.4	5
3	7.8	0.88		0	2.6	0.098	25	67	0.9968	3.2	0.68	9.8	5
4	7.8	0.76	0.04	2.3	0.092	15	54	0.997	3.26	0.65	9.8	5
5	11.2	0.28	0.56	1.9	0.075	17	60	0.998	3.16	0.58	9.8	6
6	7.4	0.7		0	1.9	0.076	11	34	0.9978	3.51	0.56	9.4	5
7	7.4	0.66		0	1.8	0.075	13	40	0.9978	3.51	0.56	9.4	5
8	7.9	0.6	0.06	1.6	0.069	15	59	0.9964	3.3	0.46	9.4	5
9	7.3	0.65		0	1.2	0.065	15	21	0.9946	3.39	0.47	10	7
10	7.8	0.58	0.02		2	0.073	9	18	0.9968	3.36	0.57	9.5	7
11	7.5	0.5	0.36	6.1	0.071	17	102	0.9978	3.35	0.8	10.5	5
12	6.7	0.58	0.08	1.8	0.097	15	65	0.9959	3.28	0.54	9.2	5
13	7.5	0.5	0.36	6.1	0.071	17	102	0.9978	3.35	0.8	10.5	5
14	5.6	0.615		0	1.6	0.089	16	59	0.9943	3.58	0.52	9.9	5
15	7.8	0.61	0.29	1.6	0.114	9	29	0.9974	3.26	1.56	9.1	5
16	8.9	0.62	0.18	3.8	0.176	52	145	0.9986	3.16	0.88	9.2	5
17	8.9	0.62	0.19	3.9	0.17	51	148	0.9986	3.17	0.93	9.2	5
18	8.5	0.28	0.56	1.8	0.092	35	103	0.9969	3.3	0.75	10.5	7
19	8.1	0.56	0.28	1.7	0.368	16	56	0.9968	3.11	1.28	9.3	5
20	7.4	0.59	0.08	4.4	0.086	6	29	0.9974	3.38	0.5	9	4

In general, the `readdlm` function is used to read in the data from the CSV files:

```
# code in Chapter 8\csv_files.jl:
fname = "winequality.csv"
data = readdlm(fname, ';')
```

The second argument is the delimiter character (here, it is `;`). The resulting data is a `1600x12 Array{Any,2}` array of the type `Any` because no common type could be found:

"fixed acidity"	"volatile acidity"	"alcohol"	"quality"
7.4	0.7	9.4	5.0
7.8	0.88	9.8	5.0
7.8	0.76	9.8	5.0

...

If the `data` file is comma separated, reading it is even simpler with the following command:

```
data2 = readcsv(fname)
```

The problem with what we have done until now is that the headers (the column titles) were read as part of the data. Fortunately, we can pass the argument `header=true` to let Julia put the first line in a separate array. It then naturally gets the correct datatype, Float64, for the data array. We can also specify the type explicitly, such as this:

```
data3 = readdlm(fname, ';', Float64, '\n', header=true)
```

The third argument here is the type of data, which is a numeric type, `String` or `Any`. The next argument is the line separator character, and the fifth indicates whether or not there is a header line with the field (column) names. If so, then `data3` is a tuple with the data as the first element and the header as the second, in our case, (1599x12 `Array{Float64,2}`, 1x12 `Array{String,2}`) (There are other optional arguments to define `readdlm`, see the `help` option). In this case, the actual data is given by `data3[1]` and the header by `data3[2]`.

Let's continue working with the variable data. The data forms a matrix, and we can get the rows and columns of data using the normal array-matrix syntax (refer to the *Matrices* section in *Chapter 5, Collection Types*). For example, the third row is given by `row3 = data[3, :]` with data: 7.8   0.88   0.0   2.6   0.098   25.0   67.0   0.9968   3.2   0.68   9.8   5.0, representing the measurements for all the characteristics of a certain wine.

The measurements of a certain characteristic for all wines are given by a `data` column, for example, `col3 = data[ :, 3]` represents the measurements of citric acid and returns a column vector 1600-element `Array{Any,1}`:   "citric acid" 0.0   0.0   0.04   0.56   0.0   0.0 ...   0.08   0.08   0.1   0.13   0.12   0.47.

If we need columns 2-4 (`volatile acidity` to `residual sugar`) for all wines, extract the data with `x = data[:, 2:4]`. If we need these measurements only for the wines on rows 70-75, get these with `y = data[70:75, 2:4]`, returning a 6 x 3 `Array{Any,2}` output as follows:

```
0.32    0.57   2.0
0.705   0.05   1.9

...

0.675   0.26   2.1
```

To get a matrix with the data from columns 3, 6, and 11, execute the following command:

```
z = [data[:,3] data[:,6] data[:,11]]
```

It would be useful to create a type `Wine` in the code.

For example, if the data is to be passed around functions, it will improve the code quality to encapsulate all the data in a single data type, like this:

```
type Wine
    fixed_acidity::Array{Float64}
    volatile_acidity::Array{Float64}
    citric_acid::Array{Float64}
    # other fields
    quality::Array{Float64}
end
```

Then, we can create objects of this type to work with them, like in any other object-oriented language, for example, `wine1 = Wine(data[1, :]...)`, where the elements of the row are splatted with the `...` operator into the `Wine` constructor.

To write to a CSV file, the simplest way is to use the `writecsv` function for a comma separator, or the `writedlm` function if you want to specify another separator. For example, to write an array `data` to a file `partial.dat`, you need to execute the following command:

```
writedlm("partial.dat", data, ';')
```

If more control is necessary, you can easily combine the more basic functions from the previous section. For example, the following code snippet writes 10 tuples of three numbers each to a file:

```
// code in Chapter 8\tuple_csv.jl
fname = "savetuple.csv"
csvfile = open(fname,"w")
# writing headers:
write(csvfile, "ColName A, ColName B, ColName C\n")
for i = 1:10
  tup(i) = tuple(rand(Float64,3)...)
  write(csvfile, join(tup(i),","), "\n")
end
close(csvfile)
```

Using DataFrames

If you measure n variables (each of a different type) of a single object of observation, then you get a table with n columns for each object row. If there are m observations, then we have m rows of data. For example, given the student grades as data, you might want to know "compute the average grade for each socioeconomic group", where grade and socioeconomic group are both columns in the table, and there is one row per student.

The DataFrame is the most natural representation to work with such a (m x n) table of data. They are similar to pandas DataFrames in Python or data.frame in R. A DataFrame is a more specialized tool than a normal array for working with tabular and statistical data, and it is defined in the DataFrames package, a popular Julia library for statistical work. Install it in your environment by typing in Pkg. add("DataFrames") in the REPL. Then, import it into your current workspace with using DataFrames. Do the same for the packages DataArrays and RDatasets (which contains a collection of example datasets mostly used in the R literature).

A common case in statistical data is that data values can be missing (the information is not known). The DataArrays package provides us with the unique value NA, which represents a missing value, and has the type NAtype. The result of the computations that contain the NA values mostly cannot be determined, for example, 42 + NA returns NA. (Julia v0.4 also has a new Nullable{T} type, which allows you to specify the type of a missing value). A DataArray{T} array is a data structure that can be n-dimensional, behaves like a standard Julia array, and can contain values of the type T, but it can also contain the missing (**Not Available**) values NA and can work efficiently with them. To construct them, use the @data macro:

```
// code in Chapter 8\dataarrays.jl
using DataArrays
using DataFrames
dv = @data([7, 3, NA, 5, 42])
```

This returns 5-element DataArray{Int64,1}: 7 3 NA 5 42.

The sum of these numbers is given by sum(dv) and returns NA. One can also assign the NA values to the array with dv[5] = NA; then, dv becomes [7, 3, NA, 5, NA]). Converting this data structure to a normal array fails: convert(Array, dv) returns ERROR: NAException.

How to get rid of these NA values, supposing we can do so safely? We can use the dropna function, for example, sum(dropna(dv)) returns 15. If you know that you can replace them with a value v, use the array function:

```
repl = -1
sum(array(dv, repl)) # returns 13
```

A DataFrame is a kind of an in-memory database, versatile in the ways you can work with the data. It consists of columns with names such as Col1, Col2, Col3, and so on. Each of these columns are DataArrays that have their own type, and the data they contain can be referred to by the column names as well, so we have substantially more forms of indexing. Unlike two-dimensional arrays, columns in a DataFrame can be of different types. One column might, for instance, contain the names of students and should therefore be a string. Another column could contain their age and should be an integer.

We construct a DataFrame from the program data as follows:

```
// code in Chapter 8\dataframes.jl
using DataFrames
# constructing a DataFrame:
df = DataFrame()
df[:Col1] = 1:4
df[:Col2] = [e, pi, sqrt(2), 42]
df[:Col3] = [true, false, true, false]
show(df)
```

Notice that the column headers are used as symbols. This returns the following 4 x 3 DataFrame object:

```
show(df)
4x3 DataFrame
| Row | Col1 | Col2    | Col3  |
|-----|------|---------|-------|
| 1   | 1    | 2.71828 | true  |
| 2   | 2    | 3.14159 | false |
| 3   | 3    | 1.41421 | true  |
| 4   | 4    | 42.0    | false |
```

We could also have used the full constructor as follows:

```
df = DataFrame(Col1 = 1:4, Col2 = [e, pi, sqrt(2), 42],
    Col3 = [true, false, true, false])
```

You can refer to the columns either by an index (the column number) or by a name, both of the following expressions return the same output:

```
show(df[2])
show(df[:Col2])
```

This gives the following output:

```
[2.718281828459045, 3.141592653589793, 1.4142135623730951,42.0]
```

To show the rows or subsets of rows and columns, use the familiar splice (:) syntax, for example:

- To get the first row, execute `df[1, :]`. This returns `1x3 DataFrame`.

Row	Col1	Col2	Col3
1	1	2.71828	true

- To get the second and third row, execute `df [2:3, :]`

- To get only the second column from the previous result, execute `df[2:3, :Col2]`. This returns `[3.141592653589793, 1.4142135623730951]`.

- To get the second and third column from the second and third row, execute `df[2:3, [:Col2, :Col3]]`, which returns the following output:

  `2x2 DataFrame`

Row	Col2	Col3
1	3.14159	false
2	1.41421	true

The following functions are very useful when working with `DataFrames`:

- The `head(df)` and `tail(df)` functions show you the first six and the last six lines of data respectively.

- The `names` function gives the names of the columns `names(df)`. It returns `3-element Array{Symbol,1}:  :Col1   :Col2   :Col3`.

- The `eltypes` function gives the data types of the columns `eltypes(df)`. It gives the output as `3-element Array{Type{T<:Top},1}:   Int64   Float64   Bool`.

- The `describe` function tries to give some useful summary information about the data in the columns, depending on the type, for example, `describe(df)` gives for column 2 (which is numeric) the min, max, median, mean, number, and percentage of NAs:

```
Col2
Min       1.4142135623730951
1st Qu.   2.392264761937558
 Median   2.929937241024419
Mean      12.318522011105483
 3rd Qu.  12.856194490192344
Max       42.0
NAs       0
NA%       0.0%
```

To load in data from a local CSV file, use the method `readtable`. The returned object is of type `DataFrame`:

```
// code in Chapter 8\dataframes.jl
using DataFrames
fname = "winequality.csv"
data = readtable(fname, separator = ';')
typeof(data) # DataFrame
size(data) # (1599,12)
```

Here is a fraction of the output:

```
1599x12 DataFrame
| Row  | fixed_acidity | volatile_acidity | citric_acid | residual_sugar |
|------|---------------|------------------|-------------|----------------|
| 1    | 7.4           | 0.7              | 0.0         | 1.9            |
| 2    | 7.8           | 0.88             | 0.0         | 2.6            |
| 3    | 7.8           | 0.76             | 0.04        | 2.3            |
:
| 1596 | 5.9           | 0.55             | 0.1         | 2.2            |
| 1597 | 6.3           | 0.51             | 0.13        | 2.3            |
| 1598 | 5.9           | 0.645            | 0.12        | 2.0            |
| 1599 | 6.0           | 0.31             | 0.47        | 3.6            |
```

The `readtable` method also supports reading in gzipped CSV files.

Writing a DataFrame to a file can be done with the `writetable` function, which takes the filename and the DataFrame as arguments, for example, `writetable("dataframe1.csv", df)`. By default, `writetable` will use the delimiter specified by the filename extension and write the column names as headers.

Both `readtable` and `writetable` support numerous options for special cases. Refer to the docs for more information (refer to `http://dataframesjl.readthedocs.org/en/latest/`). To demonstrate some of the power of DataFrames, here are some queries you can do:

- Make a vector with only the quality information `data[:quality]`
- Give the wines with alcohol percentage equal to `9.5`, for example, `data[data[:alcohol] .== 9.5, :]`

  Here, we use the `.==` operator, which does element-wise comparison. `data[:alcohol] .== 9.5` returns an array of Boolean values (true for datapoints, where `:alcohol` is `9.5`, and false otherwise). `data[boolean_array, :]` selects those rows where `boolean_array` is true.

- Count the number of wines grouped by quality with `by(data, :quality, data -> size(data, 1))`, which returns the following:

```
6x2 DataFrame

| Row | quality | x1  |
|-----|---------|-----|
| 1   | 3       | 10  |
| 2   | 4       | 53  |
| 3   | 5       | 681 |
| 4   | 6       | 638 |
| 5   | 7       | 199 |
| 6   | 8       | 18  |
```

The `DataFrames` package contains the `by` function, which takes in three arguments:

- A `DataFrame`, here it takes `data`
- A column to split the `DataFrame` on, here it takes `quality`
- A function or an expression to apply to each subset of the DataFrame, here `data -> size(data, 1)`, which gives us the number of wines for each quality value

Another easy way to get the distribution among quality is to execute the histogram `hist` function `hist(data[:quality])` that gives the counts over the range of quality (`2.0:1.0:8.0, [10,53,681,638,199,18]`). More precisely, this is a tuple with the first element corresponding to the edges of the histogram bins, and the second denoting the number of items in each bin. So there are, for example, 10 wines with quality between 2 and 3, and so on.

To extract the counts as a variable `count` of type `Vector`, we can execute `_, count = hist(data[:quality]);` the `_` means that we neglect the first element of the tuple. To obtain the quality classes as a `DataArray` class, we will execute the following:

```
class = sort(unique(data[:quality]))
```

We can now construct a `df_quality` DataFrame with the `class` and `count` columns as `df_quality = DataFrame(qual=class, no=count)`. This gives the following output:

```
6x2 DataFrame
| Row | qual | no  |
|-----|------|-----|
| 1   | 3    | 10  |
| 2   | 4    | 53  |
| 3   | 5    | 681 |
| 4   | 6    | 638 |
| 5   | 7    | 199 |
| 6   | 8    | 18  |
```

In the *Using Gadfly on data* section of *Chapter 10, The Standard Library and Packages*, we will see how to visualize `DataFrames`.

To deepen your understanding and learn about the other features of Julia DataFrames (such as joining, reshaping, and sorting), refer to the documentation available at `http://dataframesjl.readthedocs.org/en/latest/`.

Other file formats

Julia can work with other human-readable file formats through specialized packages:

- For JSON, use the `JSON` package. The `parse` method converts the JSON strings into Dictionaries, and the `json` method turns any Julia object into a JSON string.
- For XML, use the `LightXML` package
- For YAML, use the `YAML` package

- For HDF5 (a common format for scientific data), use the HDF5 package
- For working with Windows INI files, use the IniFile package

Working with TCP sockets and servers

To send data over a network, the data has to conform to a certain format or protocol. The **Transmission Control Protocol (TCP/IP)** is one of the core protocols to be used on the Internet. The following screenshot shows how to communicate over TCP/IP between a Julia Tcp server and a client (see the code in Chapter 8\tcpserver.jl):

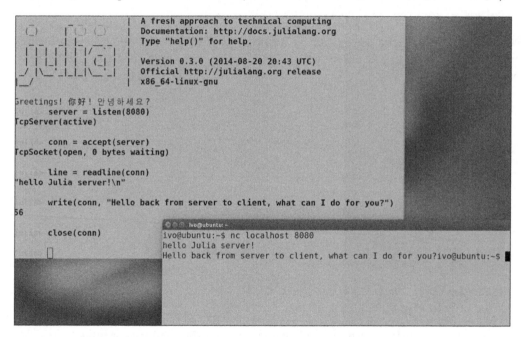

The server (in the upper-left corner) is started in a Julia session with server = listen(8080) that returns a TcpServer object listening on the port 8080. The line conn = accept(server) waits for an incoming client to make a connection. Now, in a second terminal (in the lower-right corner), start the **netcat (nc)** tool at the prompt to make a connection with the Julia server on port 8080, for example, nc localhost 8080. Then, the accept function creates a TcpSocket object on which the server can read or write.

Then, the server issues the command `line = readline(conn)`, blocking the server until it gets a full line (ending with a newline character) from the client. The client types `"hello Julia server!"` followed by *ENTER*, which appears at the server console. The server can also write text to the client over the TCP connection with the `write(conn, "message ")` function, which then appears at the client side. The server can, when finished, close the `TcpSocket` connection to close the TCP connection with `close(conn)`; this also closes the `netcat` session.

Of course, a normal server must be able to handle multiple clients. Here, you can see the code for a server that echoes back to the clients everything they send to the server:

```
// code in Chapter8\echoserver.jl
server = listen(8081)
while true
  conn = accept(server)
  @async begin
    try
      while true
        line = readline(conn)
        println(line)   # output in server console
        write(conn,line)
      end
    catch ex
      print("connection ended with error $ex")
    end
  end # end coroutine block
end
```

To achieve this, we place the `accept()` function within an infinite `while` loop, so that each incoming connection is accepted. The same is true for reading and writing to a specific client; the server only stops listening to that client when the client disconnects. Because the network communication with the clients is a possible source of errors, we have to surround it within a `try`/`catch` expression. When an error occurs, it is bound to the `ex` object. For example, when a client terminal exits, you get the `connection ended with error ErrorException("stream is closed or unusable")` message.

However, we also see a `@async` macro here, what is its function? The `@async` macro starts a new coroutine (refer to the *Tasks* section in *Chapter 4, Control Flow*) in the local process to handle the execution of the `begin-end` block that starts right after it. So, the macro `@async` handles the connection with each particular client in a separate coroutine. Thus, the `@async` block returns immediately, enabling the server to continue accepting new connections through the outer `while` loop. Because coroutines have a very low overhead, making a new one for each connection is perfectly acceptable. If it weren't for the `async` block, the program would block it until it was done with its current client before accepting a new connection.

On the other hand, the `@sync` macro is used to enclose a number of `@async` (or `@spawn` or `@parallel` calls, refer to the *Parallel operations and computing* section), and the code execution waits at the end of the `@sync` block until all the enclosed calls are finished.

Start this server example by typing the following command:

```
julia echoserver.jl
```

We can experiment with a number of netcat sessions in separate terminals. Client sessions can also be made by typing in a Julia console:

```
conn = connect(8081) #> TcpSocket(open, 0 bytes waiting)
    write(conn, "Do you hear me?\n")
```

The `listen` function has some variants, for example, `listen(IPv6(0),2001)` creates a TCP server that listens on port `2001` on all IPv6 interfaces. Similarly, instead of `readline`, there are also simpler `read` methods:

- `read(conn, Uint8)`: This method blocks until there is a byte to read from conn, and then returns it. Use `convert(Char, n)` to convert a `Uint8` value into `Char`. This will let you see the ASCII letter for `Uint8` you read in.

- `read(conn, Char)`: This method blocks until there is a byte to read from conn, and then returns it.

The important aspect about the communication API is that the code looks like the synchronous code executing line by line, even though the I/O is actually happening asynchronously through the use of tasks. We don't have to worry about writing callbacks as in some other languages. For more details about the possible methods, refer to the *I/O and Network* section at `http://docs.julialang.org/en/latest/stdlib/base/`.

Interacting with databases

Open Database Connectivity (ODBC) is a low-level protocol for establishing connections with the majority of databases and datasources (for more details, refer to `http://en.wikipedia.org/wiki/Open_Database_Connectivity`).

Julia has an `ODBC` package that enables Julia scripts to talk to ODBC data sources. Install the package through `Pkg.add("ODBC")`, and at the start of the code, run `using ODBC`.

The package can work with a system **Data Source Name (DSN)** that contains all the concrete connection information, such as server name, database, credentials, and so on. Every operating system has its own utility to make DSNs. In Windows, the ODBC administrator can be reached by navigating to **Configuration | System Administration | ODBC Data Sources**; on other systems, you have IODBC or Unix ODBC.

For example, suppose we have a database called `pubs` running in a SQL Server or a MySQL Server, and the connection is described with a DSN `pubsODBC`. Now, I can connect to this database as follows:

```
// code in Chapter 8\odbc.jl
using ODBC
ODBC.connect("pubsODBC")
```

This returns an output as follows:

```
ODBC Connection Object
----------------------
Connection Data Source: pubsODBC
pubsODBC Connection Number: 1
    Contains resultset? No
```

You can also store this connection object in a variable `conn` as follows:

```
conn = ODBC.connect("pubsODBC")
```

This way, you are able to close the connection when necessary through `disconnect(conn)` to save the database resources, or handle multiple connections.

To launch a query on the `titles` table, you only need to use the `query` function as follows:

```
results = query("select * from titles")
```

The result is of the type DataFrame and dimensions 18 x 10, because the table contains 18 rows and 10 columns, for example, here are some of the columns:

```
| Row | title                                                   |
|-----|---------------------------------------------------------|
| 1   | "The Busy Executive's Database Guide"                   |
| 2   | "Cooking with Computers: Surreptitious Balance Sheets"  |
| 3   | "You Can Combat Computer Stress!"                       |
| 4   | "Straight Talk About Computers"                         |
| 5   | "Silicon Valley Gastronomic Treats"                     |
| 6   | "The Gourmet Microwave"                                 |

| Row | _type          | pub_id  | price | advance | royalty | ytd_sales |
|-----|----------------|---------|-------|---------|---------|-----------|
| 1   | "business    " | "1389"  | 19.99 | 5000.0  | 10      | 4095      |
| 2   | "business    " | "1389"  | 11.95 | 5000.0  | 10      | 3876      |
| 3   | "business    " | "0736"  | 2.99  | 10125.0 | 24      | 18722     |
| 4   | "business    " | "1389"  | 19.99 | 5000.0  | 10      | 4095      |
| 5   | "mod_cook    " | "0877"  | 19.99 | 0.0     | 12      | 2032      |
| 6   | "mod_cook    " | "0877"  | 2.99  | 15000.0 | 24      | 22246     |
```

If you haven't stored the query results in a variable, you can always retrieve them from conn.resultset, where conn is an existing connection. Now we have all the functionalities of DataFrames at our disposal to work with this data. Launching data manipulation queries works in the same way:

```
updsql = "update titles set type = 'psychology' where
    title_id='BU1032'"
query(updsql)
```

When successful, the result is a 0x0 DataFrame. In order to see which ODBC drivers are installed on the system, ask for listdrivers(). The already available DSNs are listed with listdsns().

Julia already has database drivers for Memcache, FoundationDB, MongoDB, Redis, MySQL, SQLite, and PostgreSQL (for more information, refer to https://github. com/svaksha/Julia.jl/blob/master/Database.md#postgresql).

Parallel operations and computing

In our multicore CPU and clustered computing world, it is imperative for a new language to have excellent parallel computing capabilities. This is one of the main strengths of Julia, providing an environment based on message passing between multiple processes that can execute on the same machine or on remote machines. In that sense, it implements the actor model (as Erlang, Elixir, and Dart do), but we'll see that the actual coding happens on a higher level than receiving and sending messages between processes, or workers (processors) as Julia calls them. The developer only needs to manage explicitly the main process from which all other workers are started. The message send and receive operations are simulated by higher-level operations that look like function calls.

Creating processes

Julia can be started as a REPL or as a separate application with a number of workers n available. The following command starts n processes on the local machine:

```
// code in Chapter 8\parallel.jl
julia -p n   # starts REPL with n workers
```

These workers are different processes, not threads, so they do not share memory.

To get the most out of a machine, set n equal to the number of processor cores. For example, when n is 8, then you have, in fact, 9 workers: one for the REPL shell itself, and eight others that are ready to do parallel tasks. Every worker has its own integer identifier, which we can see by calling the workers function workers(). This returns the following:

```
8-element Array{Int64,1} containing:   2  3  4  5  6  7  8  9
```

Process 1 is the REPL worker. We can now iterate over the workers with the following command:

```
for pid in workers()
  # do something with each process (pid = process id)
end
```

Each worker can get its own process ID with the function myid(). If at a certain moment, you need more workers, adding new ones is easy:

```
addprocs(5)
```

This returns `5-element Array{Any,1}` that contains their process identifiers `10 11 12 13 14`. The default method adds workers on the local machine, but the `addprocs` method accepts arguments to start processes on remote machines via SSH. This is the secure shell protocol that enables you to execute commands on a remote computer via a shell in a totally encrypted manner.

The number of available workers is given by `nprocs()`, in our case, this is `14`. A worker can be removed by calling `rmprocs()` with its identifier, for example, `rmprocs(3)` stops the worker with ID `3`.

All these workers communicate via TCP ports and run on the same machine, which is why it is called a local cluster. To activate workers on a cluster of computers, start Julia as follows:

```
julia --machinefile machines driver.jl
```

Here, `machines` is a file that contains the names of the computers you want to engage, like this:

```
node01
node01
node02
node02
node03
```

Here `node01`, `node02`, and `node03` are the three names of computers in the cluster, and we want to start two workers each on `node01` and `node02`, and one worker on `node03`.

The `driver.jl` file is the script that runs the calculations and has the process identifier `1`. This command uses a password-less SSH login to start the worker processes on the specified machines. The following screenshot shows all the eight processors on an eight core machine when engaged in a parallel operation:

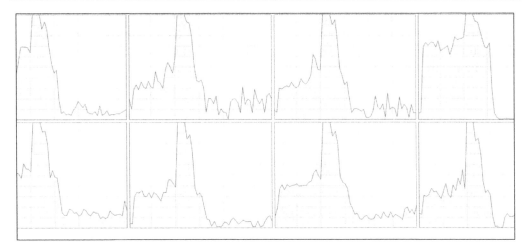

The horizontal axis is time, and the vertical is the CPU usage. On each core, a worker process is engaged in a long-running Fibonacci calculation.

Processors can be dynamically added or removed to a master Julia process, both locally on symmetric multiprocessor systems, remotely on a computer cluster as well as in the cloud. If more versatility is needed, you can work with the ClusterManager type (see http://docs.julialang.org/en/latest/manual/parallel-computing/).

Using low-level communications

Julia's native parallel computing model is based on two primitives: **remote calls** and **remote references**. At this level, we can give a certain worker a function with arguments to execute with remotecall, and get the result back with fetch. As a trivial example in the following code, we call upon worker 2 to execute a square function on the number 1000:

```
r1 = remotecall(2, x -> x^2, 1000)
```

This returns RemoteRef(2,1,20).

The arguments are: the worker ID, the function, and the function's arguments. Such a remote call returns immediately, thus not blocking the main worker (the REPL in this case). The main process continues executing while the remote worker does the assigned job. The remotecall function returns a variable r1 of type RemoteRef, which is a reference to the computed result, that we can get using fetch:

```
fetch(r1) which returns  1000000
```

The call to `fetch` will block the main process until worker 2 has finished the calculation. The main processor can also run `wait(r1)`, which also blocks until the result of the remote call becomes available. If you need the remote result immediately in the local operation, use the following command:

```
remotecall_fetch(5, sin, 2pi) which  returns -2.4492935982947064e-16
```

This is more efficient than `fetch(remotecall(..))`.

You can also use the `@spawnat` macro that evaluates the expression in the second argument on the worker specified by the first argument:

```
r2 = @spawnat 4 sqrt(2) # lets worker 4 calculate sqrt(2)
  fetch(r2)  # returns 1.4142135623730951
```

This is made even easier with `@spawn`, which only needs an expression to evaluate, because it decides for itself where it will be executed: `r3 = @spawn sqrt(5)` returns `RemoteRef(5,1,26)` and `fetch(r3)` returns `2.23606797749979`.

To execute a certain function on all the workers, we can use a comprehension:

```
r = [@spawnat w sqrt(5) for w in workers()]
  fetch(r[3]) # returns 2.23606797749979
```

To execute the same statement on all the workers, we can also use the `@everywhere` macro:

```
@everywhere println(myid()) 1
          From worker 2:   2
          From worker 3:   3
          From worker 4:   4
          From worker 7:   7
          From worker 5:   5
          From worker 6:   6
          From worker 8:   8
          From worker 9:   9
```

All the workers correspond to different processes; they therefore do not share variables, for example:

```
x = 5 #> 5
@everywhere println(x) #> 5
  # exception on 2 exception on : 4: ERROR: x not defined ...
```

The variable x is only known in the main process, all the other workers return the
ERROR: x not defined error message.

@everywhere can also be used to make the data like the variable w that is available to
all processors, for example, @everywhere w = 8.

The following example makes a source file defs.jl available to all the workers:

```
@everywhere include("defs.jl")
```

Or more explicitly a function fib(n) as follows:

```
@everywhere function fib(n)
  if (n < 2) then
    return n
  else return fib(n-1) + fib(n-2)
  end
end
```

In order to be able to perform its task, a remote worker needs access to the function
it executes. You can make sure that all workers know about the functions they need
by loading the source code functions.jl with require, making it available to all
workers:

```
require("functions")
```

In a cluster, the contents of this file (and any files loaded recursively) will be sent
over the network.

A best practice is to separate your code into two files: one file (functions.jl) that
contains the functions and parameters that need to be run in parallel, and the other
file (driver.jl) that manages the processing and collecting the results. Use the
require("functions") command in driver.jl to import the functions and
parameters to all processors.

An alternative is to specify the files to load on the command line. If you need the
source files file1.jl and file2.jl on all the n processors at start-up time, use the
syntax julia -p n -L file1.jl -L file2.jl driver.jl, where driver.jl is
the script that organizes the computations.

Data movement between workers (such as when calling fetch) needs to be reduced
as much as possible in order to get performance and scalability.

If every worker needs to know a variable d, this can be broadcast to all processes with the following code:

```
for pid in workers()
    remotecall(pid, x -> (global d; d = x; nothing), d)
end
```

Each worker then has its local copy of data. Scheduling of the workers is done with tasks (refer to the *Tasks* section of *Chapter 4, Control Flow*), so that no locking is required, for example, when a communication operation such as fetch or wait is executed, the current task is suspended, and the scheduler picks another task to run. When the wait event completes (for example, the data shows up), the current task is restarted.

In many cases, however, you do not have to specify or create processes to do parallel programming in Julia, as we will see in the next section.

Parallel loops and maps

A for loop with a large number of iterations is a good candidate for parallel execution, and Julia has a special construct to do this: the @parallel macro, which can be used for the for loops and comprehensions.

Let's calculate an approximation for π using the famous Buffon's needle problem. If we drop a needle onto a floor with equal parallel strips of wood, what is the probability that the needle will cross a line between two strips? Let's take a look at the following screenshot:

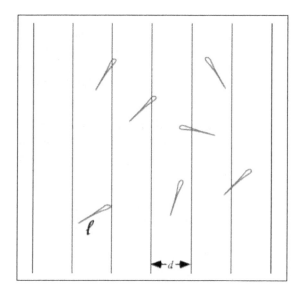

Without getting into the mathematical intricacies of this problem (if you are interested, see http://en.wikipedia.org/wiki/Buffon's_needle), a function buffon(n) can be deduced from the model assumptions that return an approximation for π when throwing the needle n times (assuming the length of the needle 1 and the width d between the strips both equal to 1):

```
// code in Chapter 8\parallel_loops_maps.jl
function buffon(n)
  hit = 0
  for i = 1:n
    mp = rand()
    phi = (rand() * pi) - pi / 2 # angle at which needle falls
    xright = mp + cos(phi)/2 # x location of needle
    xleft = mp - cos(phi)/2
    # does needle cross either x == 0 or x == 1?
    p = (xright >= 1 || xleft <= 0) ? 1 : 0
    hit += p
  end
  miss = n - hit
  piapprox = n / hit * 2
end
```

With ever increasing n, the calculation time increases, because the number of the for iterations that have to be executed in one thread on one processor increases, but we also get a better estimate for π:

```
@time buffon(100000)
```

```
elapsed time: 0.005487779 seconds (96 bytes allocated)
  3.1467321186947355
```

```
@time buffon(100000000)
```

```
elapsed time: 5.362294859 seconds (96 bytes allocated)
  3.1418351308191026
```

However, what if we could spread the calculations over the available processors? For this, we have to rearrange our code a bit. In the sequential version, the variable hit is increased on every iteration inside the for loop with the amount p (which is 0 or 1). In the parallel version, we rewrite the code, so that this p is exactly the result of the for loop (one calculation) done on one of the processors engaged.

Julia also provides a `@parallel` macro that acts on a `for` loop, splitting the range, and distributing it to each process. It optionally takes a "reducer" as its first argument. If a reducer is specified, the results from each remote procedure will be aggregated using the reducer. In the following example, we use the `(+)` function as a reducer, which means that the last values of the parallel blocks on each worker will be summed to calculate the final value of hit:

```
function buffon_par(n)
  hit = @parallel (+) for i = 1:n
      mp = rand()
      phi = (rand() * pi) - pi / 2
      xright = mp + cos(phi)/2
      xleft = mp - cos(phi)/2
        (xright >= 1 || xleft <= 0) ? 1 : 0
    end
  miss = n - hit
  piapprox = n / hit * 2
end
```

On my machine with eight processors, this gives the following results:

```
@time buffon_par(100000)
elapsed time: 0.005903334 seconds (296920 bytes allocated)
  3.136762860727729
@time buffon_par(100000000)
elapsed time: 0.849702686 seconds (300888 bytes allocated)
  3.141665751394711
```

We see much better performance for the higher number of iterations (a factor of `6.3` in this case). By changing a normal `for` loop into a parallel reducing version, we were able to get substantial improvements in the calculation time, at the cost of higher memory consumption. In general, always test whether the parallel version really is an improvement over the sequential version in your specific case!

The first argument of `@parallel` is the reducing operator (here, `(+)`), the second is the `for` loop, which must start on the same line. The calculations in the loop must be independent from one another, because the order in which they run is arbitrary, given that they are scheduled over the different workers. The actual reduction (summing up in this case) is done on the calling process.

Any variables used inside the parallel loop will be copied (broadcasted) to each process. Because of this, the code like the following will fail to initialize the array `arr`, because each process has a copy of it:

```
arr = zeros(100000)
@parallel for i=1:100000
  arr[i] = i
end
```

After the loop, `arr` still contains all the zeros, because it is the copy on the master worker.

If the computational task is to apply a function to all elements in some collection, you can use a **parallel map** operation through the `pmap` function. The `pmap` function takes the following form: `pmap(f, coll)`, applies a function `f` on each element of the collection `coll` in parallel, but preserves the order of the collection in the result. Suppose we have to calculate the rank of a number of large matrices. We can do this sequentially as follows:

```
function rank_marray()
  marr = [rand(1000,1000) for i=1:10]
  for arr in marr
      println(rank(arr))
  end
end

@time rank_marray() # prints out ten times 1000
elapsed time: 4.351479797 seconds (166177728 bytes allocated,
  1.43% gc time)
```

Here, parallelizing also gives benefits (a factor of `1.6`):

```
function prank_marray()
  marr = [rand(1000,1000) for i=1:10]
  println(pmap(rank, marr))
end
@time prank_marray()
elapsed time: 2.785466798 seconds (163955848 bytes allocated, 1.96% gc
time)
```

The `@parallel` macro and `pmap` are both powerful tools to tackle **map-reduce** problems.

Distributed arrays

When computations have to be done on a very large array (or arrays), the array can be distributed, so that each process works in parallel on a different part of the array. In this way, we can make use of the memory resources of multiple machines, and allow the manipulation of arrays that would be too large to fit on one machine.

The specific data type used here is called a **distributed array** or **DArray**; most operations behave exactly as on the normal Array type, so the parallelism is invisible. With DArray, each process has local access to just a part of the data, and no two processes share the same data. For example, the following code creates a distributed array of random numbers with dimensions 100 x 100 and is divided over four workers. The data division given by the third argument says to divide the number of columns evenly over the four workers:

```
// code in Chapter 8\distrib_arrays.jl:
arr = drand((100,100), workers()[1:4], [1,4])
    100x100 DArray{Float64,2,Array{Float64,2}}: …
```

The following properties of the DArray arr makes this clear:

```
 arr.pmap # on which workers ? 4-element Array{Int64,1}: 2 3 4 5
```

```
arr.indexes #  which worker has which data indices1x4
  Array{(UnitRange{Int64},UnitRange{Int64}),2}:
```

```
 (1:100,1:25)   (1:100,26:50)   (1:100,51:75)   (1:100,76:100)
```

```
arr.cuts #  where the data is partitioned
```

```
2-element Array{Array{Int64,1},1}:
```

```
 [1,101]
```

```
 [1, 26, 51, 76, 101]
```

```
arr.chunks # references on the workers:
```

```
1x4 Array{RemoteRef,2}:
```

```
RemoteRef(2,1,11164)   RemoteRef(3,1,11165)   …   RemoteRef(5,1,11167)
```

DArrays can also be created with the @parallel macro as follows:

```
da = @parallel [2i for i = 1:10]
```

```
# 10-element DArray{Int64,1,Array{Int64,1}}: …
```

The following code snippet is often used to construct a distributed array divided over the available workers:

```
DArray((10,10)) do I
    println(I)
    return zeros(length(I[1]),length(I[2]))
end
```

(I is a tuple of index ranges, which is constructed automatically).

This returns the following output of a 10x10 array filled with zeros divided over the available workers:

```
        From worker 2:    (1:5,1:3)
        From worker 8:    (1:5,9:10)
        From worker 4:    (1:5,4:5)
        From worker 3:    (6:10,1:3)
        From worker 5:    (6:10,4:5)
        From worker 7:    (6:10,6:8)
        From worker 6:    (1:5,6:8)
        From worker 9:    (6:10,9:10)
10x10 DArray{Float64,2,Array{Float64,2}}:   0.0   0.0   0.0   0.0 ....
```

For more information on distributed arrays, refer to http://docs.julialang.org/en/latest/manual/parallel-computing/#distributed-arrays.

Julia's model for building a large parallel application works by means of a global distributed address space. This means that you can hold a reference to an object that lives on another machine participating in a computation. These references are easily manipulated and passed around between machines, making it simple to keep track of what's being computed where. Also, machines can be added in mid computation when needed.

Summary

In this chapter, we explored a lot of material. We learned how the I/O system in Julia is constructed, how to work with files and DataFrames, and how to connect with databases using ODBC. The basics of network programming in Julia was also discussed, and then we got an overview of the parallel computing functionality, from the primitive operations to map-reduce functions and distributed arrays. In the next chapter, we will take a look at how Julia interacts with the command line and with other languages, and discuss some performance tips.

Running External Programs

Sometimes, your code needs to interact with programs in the outside world, be it the operating system in which it runs, or other languages such as C or FORTRAN. This chapter shows how straightforward it is to run external programs from Julia and covers the following topics:

- Running shell commands—interpolation and pipelining
- Calling C and FORTRAN
- Calling Python
- Performance tips—a summary

Running shell commands

To interact with the operating system from within the Julia REPL, there are a few helper functions available as follows:

- `pwd()`: This function prints the current directory, for example, `"d:\\test"`
- `cd("d:\\test\\week1")`: This function helps to navigate to subdirectories
- In the interactive shell, you can also use the *shell mode* using the `;` modifier:

    - `; ls`: This prints, for example, **file1.txt shell.jl test.txt tosort.txt**
    - `; mkdir folder`: This makes a directory named `folder`
    - `; cd folder`: This helps to navigate to `folder`

However, what if you want to run a shell command by the operating system (the OS)? Julia offers an efficient shell integration through the `run` function, which takes an object of type `Cmd` that is defined by enclosing a command string in backticks (` `` `):

```
# Code in Chapter 9\shell.jl:
    cmd = `echo Julia is smart`
typeof(cmd) #> Cmd
    run(cmd) # returns Julia is smart
    run(`date`) #> Sun Oct 12 09:44:50 GMT 2014
cmd = `cat file1.txt`
run(cmd) # prints the contents of file1.txt
```

 Be careful to enclose the command text in backticks (` `` `), not single quotes (`'`).

If the execution of `cmd` by the OS goes wrong, `run` throws a **failed process** error. You might want to first test the command before running it; `success(cmd)` will return true if it will execute successfully, otherwise it returns false.

Julia forks commands as **child processes** from the Julia process. Instead of immediately running the command in the shell, backticks create a `Cmd` object to represent the command, which can then be run, connected to other commands via pipes, and read or write to it.

Interpolation

String interpolation with the `$` operator is allowed in a command object like this:

```
    file = "file1.txt"
  cmd = `cat $file` # equivalent to `cat file1.txt`
  run(cmd) #> prints the contents of file1.txt
```

This is very similar to the string interpolation with `$` in strings (refer to the *Strings* section in *Chapter 2, Variables, Types, and Operations*).

Pipelining

Julia defines a pipeline operator with symbol `|>` to redirect the output of a command as the input to the following command:

```
    run(`cat $file` |> "test.txt")
```

This writes the contents of the file referred to by $file into test.txt, which is shown as follows:

```
run("test.txt" |> `cat`)
```

This pipeline operator can even be chained as follows:

```
run(`echo $("\nhi\nJulia")` |> `cat` |> `grep -n J`) #>
    3:Julia
```

If the file tosort.txt contains B A C on consecutive lines, then the following command will sort the lines:

```
run(`cat "tosort.txt"` |> `sort`) # returns A B C
```

Another example is to search for the word "is" in all the text files in the current folder; use the following command:

```
run(`grep is $(readdir())`)
```

To capture the result of a command in Julia, use readall or readline:

```
a = readall(`cat "tosort.txt"` |> `sort`)
```

Now a has the value "A\r\nB\r\nC\n".

Multiple commands can be run in parallel with the & operator:

```
run(`cat "file1.txt"` & `cat "tosort.txt"`)
```

This will print the lines of the two files intermingled, because the printing happens concurrently.

Using this functionality requires careful testing, and probably, the code will differ according to the operating system on which your Julia program runs. You can obtain the OS from the variable OS_NAME, or use the macros @windows, @unix, @linux, and @osx, which were specifically designed to handle platform variations. For example, let's say we want to execute the function fun1() if we are on Windows, else the function fun2(). We can write this as follows:

```
@windows ? fun1() : fun2()
```

Calling C and FORTRAN

While Julia can rightfully claim to obviate the need to write some C or FORTRAN code, it is possible that you will need to interact with the existing C or FORTRAN shared libraries. Functions in such a library can be called directly by Julia, with no glue code, or boilerplate code or compilation needed. Because Julia's LLVM compiler generates native code, calling a C function from Julia has exactly the same overhead as calling the same function from C code itself. However, first, we need to know a few more things:

- For calling out to C, we need to work with pointer types; a native pointer Ptr{T} is nothing more than the memory address for a variable of type T

- At this lower level, the term bitstype is also used; bitstype is a concrete type whose data consists of bits, such as Int8, Uint8, Int32, Float64, Bool, and Char

- To pass a string to C, it is converted to a contiguous byte array representation with the function bytestring(); given Ptr to a C string, it returns a Julia string.

Here is how to call a C function in a shared library (calling FORTRAN is done similarly): suppose we want to know the value of an environment variable in our system, say the language, we can obtain this by calling the C function getenv from the shared library libc:

```
# code in Chapter 9\callc.jl:
lang = ccall( (:getenv, "libc"), Ptr{Uint8}, (Ptr{Uint8},),
"LANGUAGE")
```

This returns Ptr{Uint8} @0x00007fff8d178dad. To see its string contents, execute bytestring(lang), which returns en_US.

In general, ccall takes the following arguments:

- A (:function, "library") tuple with the name of the C function (here, getenv) is used as a symbol, and the library name (here, libc) as a string

- The return type (here, Ptr{Uint8}), which can be any bitstype, or Ptr

- A tuple of types of the input arguments (here, (Ptr{Uint8})), note the tuple

- The actual arguments if there are any (here, "LANGUAGE")

It is generally advisable to test for the existence of a library before doing the call. This can be tested like this: find_library(["libc"]), which returns "libc", when the library is found or "" when it cannot find the library.

When calling a FORTRAN function, all inputs must be passed by reference. Arguments to C functions are, in general, automatically converted, and the returned values in C types are also converted to Julia types. Arrays of Booleans are handled differently in C and Julia and cannot be passed directly, so they must be manually converted. The same applies for some system dependent types (refer to the following references for more details).

The `ccall` function will also automatically ensure that all of its arguments will be preserved from garbage collection until the call returns. C types are mapped to Julia types, for example, `short` is mapped to `Int16`, and `double` to `Float64`.

A complete table of these mappings as well as a lot more intricate detail can be found in the Julia docs at `http://docs.julialang.org/en/latest/manual/calling-c-and-fortran-code/`. The other way around by calling Julia functions from C code (or embedding Julia in C) is also possible, refer to `http://docs.julialang.org/en/latest/manual/embedding/`. Julia and C can also share array data without copying. Another way that C code can call Julia code is in the form of callback functions (refer to `http://julialang.org/blog/2013/05/callback/`).

If you have the existing C code, you must compile it as a shared library to call it from Julia. With GCC, you can do this using the `-shared -fPIC` command-line arguments. Support for C++ is more limited and is provided by the `Cpp` and `Clang` packages.

Calling Python

The `PyCall` package provides for calling Python from Julia code. As always, add this package to your Julia environment with `Pkg.add("PyCall")`. Then, you can start using it in the REPL or in a script as follows:

```
using PyCall
pyeval("10*10") #> 100
@pyimport math
math.sin(math.pi / 2) #> 1.0
```

As we can see with the `@pyimport` macro, we can easily import any Python library; functions inside such a library are called with the familiar dot notation.

For more details, refer to `https://github.com/stevengj/PyCall.jl`.

Performance tips

Throughout this book, we paid attention to performance. Here, we summarize some of the highlighted performance topics and give some additional tips. These tips need not always be used, and you should always benchmark or profile the code and the effect of a tip, but applying some of them can often yield a remarkable performance improvement. Using type annotations everywhere is certainly *not* the way to go, Julia's type inferring engine does that work for you:

- **Refrain from using global variables**. If unavoidable, make them constant, or at least annotate the types. It is better to use local variables instead; they are often only kept on the stack (or even in registers), especially if they are immutable.

- Structure your code around functions that do their work on local variables via the function arguments, and this returns their results rather than mutating the global objects.

- Type stability is very important:
    - Avoid changing the types of variables over time
    - The return type of a function should only depend on the type of the arguments

    Even if you do not know the types that will be used in a function, but you do know it will always be of the same type T and U, then functions should be defined keeping that in mind, as in this code snippet:

    ```
    function myFunc{T,U}(a::T, b::U, c::Int)
      # code
    end
    ```

- If large arrays are needed, indicate their final size with `sizehint` from the start (refer to the *Ranges and Arrays* section of *Chapter 2, Variables, Types, and Operations*).

- If `arr` is a very large array that you no longer need, you can free the memory it occupies by setting `arr = nothing`. The occupied memory will be released the next time the garbage collector runs. You can force this to happen by invoking `gc()`.

- In certain cases (such as real-time applications), disabling garbage collection (temporarily) with `gc_disable()` can be useful.

- Use named functions instead of anonymous functions.

- In general, use small functions.

- Don't test for the types of arguments inside a function, use an argument type annotation instead.

- If necessary, code different versions of a function (several methods) according to the types, so that multiple dispatch applies. Normally, this won't be necessary, because the JIT compiler is optimized to deal with the types as they come.

- Use types for keyword arguments; avoid using the splat operator (...) for dynamic lists of keyword arguments.

- Using mutating APIs (functions with ! at the end) is helpful, for example, to avoid copying large arrays.

- Prefer array operations to comprehensions, for example, x.^2 is considerably faster than [val^2 for val in x].

- Don't use try/catch in the inner loop of a calculation.

- Use immutable types (cfr. package ImmutableArrays).

- Avoid using type Any, especially in collection types.

- Avoid using abstract types in a collection.

- Type annotate fields in composite types.

- Avoid using a large number of variables, large temporary arrays, and collections, because this provokes much garbage collection. Also, don't make copies of variables if you don't have to.

- Avoid using string interpolation ($) when writing to a file, just write the values.

- Devectorize your code, that is, use explicit for loops on array elements instead of simply working with the arrays and matrices. (This is exactly the opposite advice as commonly given to R, MATLAB, or Python users.)

- If appropriate, use a parallel reducing form with @parallel instead of a normal for loop (refer to *Chapter 8, I/O, Networking, and Parallel Computing*).

- Reduce data movement between workers in a parallel execution as much as possible (refer to *Chapter 8, I/O, Networking, and Parallel Computing*).

- Fix deprecation warnings.

- Use the macro @inbounds so that no array bounds checking occur in expressions (if you are absolutely certain that no BoundsError occurs!).

- Avoid using eval at runtime.

In general, split your code in functions. Data types will be determined at function calls, and when a function returns. Types that are not supplied will be inferred, but the Any type does not translate to the efficient code. If types are stable (that is, variables stick to the same type) and can be inferred, then your code will run fast.

Tools to use

Execute a function with certain parameter values, and then use @time (refer to the *Generic functions and multiple dispatch* section in *Chapter 3, Functions*) to measure the elapsed time and memory allocation. If too much memory is allocated, investigate the code for type problems.

Experiment different tips and techniques in the script array_product_benchmark. jl. Use code_typed (refer to the *Reflection capabilities* section in *Chapter 7, Metaprogramming in Julia*) to see if type Any is inferred.

There is a **linter** tool (the Lint package) that can give you all kinds of warnings and suggestions to improve your code. Use it as follows:

```
Pkg.add("Lint")
using Lint
lintfile("performance.jl")
```

This produces the output as follows:

performance.jl [   ] 33 ERROR Use of undeclared symbol a

performance.jl [with_keyword   ]   6 INFO Argument declared but not used: name

performance.jl [   ] 21 INFO A type is not given to the field name, which can be slow

Some useful type checking and type stability investigation can be done with the package TypeCheck, for example, checking the return types of a function or checking types in a loop.

A **profiler** tool is available in the standard library to measure the performance of your running code and identify possible bottleneck lines. This works through calling your code with the @profile macro (refer to http://docs.julialang.org/en/latest/stdlib/profile/#stdlib-profiling). The ProfileView package provides a nice graphical browser to investigate the profile results (follow the tutorial at https://github.com/timholy/ProfileView.jl).

For more tips, examples, and argumentation about performance, look up `http://docs.julialang.org/en/latest/manual/performance-tips/`.

A debugger can be found at `https://github.com/toivoh/Debug.jl`; it should be included in Julia v0.4.

Summary

In this chapter, we saw how easy it is to run commands at the operating system level. Interfacing with C is not that much more difficult, although it is somewhat specialized. Finally, we reviewed the best practices at our disposal to make Julia perform at its best. In the last chapter, we will get to know some of the more important packages when using Julia in real projects.

10
The Standard Library and Packages

In this final chapter of our mini tour on Julia, we look anew at the standard library and explore the ever-growing ecosystem of packages for Julia. We will discuss the following topics:

- Digging deeper into the standard library
- Julia's package manager
- Publishing a package
- Graphics in Julia
- Using Gadfly on data

Digging deeper into the standard library

The standard library is written in Julia and comprises of a very broad range of functionalities: from regular expressions, working with dates and times (in v 0.4), a package manager, internationalization and Unicode, linear algebra, complex numbers, specialized mathematical functions, statistics, I/O and networking, **Fast Fourier Transformations (FFT)**, parallel computing, to macros, and reflection. Julia provides a firm and broad foundation for numerical computing and data science (for example, much of what NumPy has to offer is provided). Despite being targeted at numerical computing and data science, Julia aims to be a general purpose programming language.

The source code of the standard library can be found in the `share\julia\base` subfolder of Julia's root installation folder. Coding in Julia leads almost naturally to this source code, for example, when viewing all the methods of a particular function with `methods()`, or when using the `@which` macro to find out more about a certain method (refer to the *Generic functions and multiple dispatch* section in *Chapter 3, Functions*). IJulia even provides hyperlinks to the source code, as shown in the following screenshot:

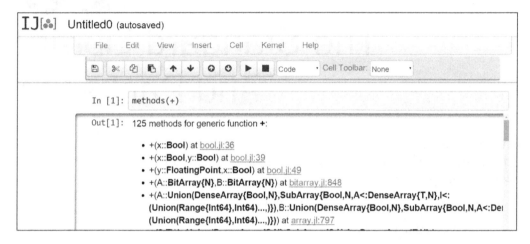

We covered some of the most important types and functions in the previous chapters, and you can refer to the manual for a more exhaustive overview at `http://docs.julialang.org/en/latest/stdlib/base/`.

It is certainly important to know that Julia contains a wealth of functional constructs to work with collections, such as the `reduce`, `fold`, `min`, `max`, `sum`, `any`, `all`, `map`, and `filter` functions. Some examples are as follows:

- `filter(f, coll)` applies the function `f` to all the elements of the collection `coll`:

  ```
  # code in Chapter 10\stdlib.jl:
  filter(x -> iseven(x), 1:10)
  ```

  This returns `5-element Array{Int64,1}` that consists of 2, 4, 6, 8, and 10.

- `mapreduce(f, op, coll)` applies the function `f` to all the elements of `coll` and then reduces this to one resulting value by applying the operation `op`:

  ```
  mapreduce(x -> sqrt(x), +, 1:10) #> 22.4682781862041
  # which is equivalent to:
  sum(map(x -> sqrt(x), 1:10))
  ```

- The pipeline operator (|>) also lets you write very functionally styled code. Using the form x |> f, it applies the function f to the argument x, and the results of this function can be chained to the following function. With this notation, we can rewrite the previous example as:

```
1:10 |> (x -> sqrt(x)) |> sum
```

Or, it can be written even shorter as follows:

```
1:10 |> sqrt |> sum
```

When working in the REPL, it can be handy to store a variable in the operating system's clipboard if you want to clean the REPL's variables memory with workspace(). Consider the ensuing example:

```
a = 42
clipboard(a)
workspace()
a # returns ERROR: a not defined
a = clipboard() # returns "42"
```

This also works while copying information from another application, for example, a string from a website or from a text editor. On Linux, you will have to install xclip with the following command:

```
sudo apt-get install xclip
```

Julia's package manager

The *Packages* section in *Chapter 1, Installing the Julia Platform*, introduced us to the Julia's package system (some 370 packages and counting) and its manager program Pkg. Most Julia libraries are written exclusively in Julia; this makes them not only more portable, but also an excellent source for learning and experimenting with Julia in your own modified versions. The packages that are useful for the data scientists are Stats, Distributions, GLM, and Optim. You can search for applicable packages in the http://pkg.julialang.org/indexorg.html repository. For a list of the packages we encountered in this book, consult the *List of Packages* section in *Appendix, List of Macros and Packages*, after this chapter.

Installing and updating packages

It is advisable to regularly (and certainly, before installing a new package) execute the `Pkg.update()` function to ensure that your local package repository is up to date and synchronized, as shown in the following screenshot:

```
        Pkg.update()
INFO: Updating METADATA...
INFO: Updating cache of JSON...
INFO: Updating cache of Winston...
INFO: Updating cache of DataArrays...
INFO: Updating cache of Distributions...
INFO: Updating ANN...
INFO: Computing changes...
```

As we saw in *Chapter 1, Installing the Julia Platform*, packages are installed via `Pkg.add("PackageName")` and brought into scope using `PackageName`. This presumes the package is published on the METADATA repository; if this is not the case, you can clone it from a `git` repository as follows: `Pkg.clone("git@github.com:EricChiang/ANN.jl.git")`.

An alternative way is to add one or more package names to the REQUIRE file in your Julia home folder, and then execute `Pkg.resolve()` to install them and their dependencies.

If you need to force a certain package to a certain version (perhaps an older version), use `Pkg.pin()`, for example, use `Pkg.pin("HDF5", v"0.4.3")` to force the use of Version `0.4.3` of package HDF5, even when you already have v 0.4.4 installed.

Publishing a package

All package management in Julia is done via GitHub. Here are the steps for publishing your own package:

1. Fork the package METADATA.`jl` on GitHub, get the address of your fork, and execute the following:

   ```
   $ git clone git@github.com:your-user-name/METADATA.jl.git
   $ cd METADATA.jl
   ```

2. Make a new branch with the following commands:

```
$ git branch mypack
$ git checkout mypack
```

3. Add the stuff for your package in a folder, say MyPack. Your code should go in a /src folder, which should also contain mypack.jl, that will be run when the command using MyPack is issued. The tests should go in the /tests folder. You should have a runtests.jl file in the folder that runs the tests for your package.

A text file named REQUIRE is where any dependencies on other Julia packages go; it is also where you specify compatible versions of Julia.

For example, it can contain the following:

```
julia 0.3-
BinDeps
@windows WinRPM
```

This certifies that this package is compatible with Julia v0.3 or higher; it needs the package BinDeps, and on Windows it needs the package WinRPM.

The license you want goes in LICENSE.md, and some documentation goes in README.md.

Then, you will have to run the following commands:

```
$ git add MyPack/*
$ git commit -m "My fabulous package"
```

4. Then, push it to GitHub:

```
$ git push --set-upstream origin mypack
```

5. Go to the GitHub website of your fork of METADATA.jl and a green button **Compare & pull request** should appear, and you're just a few clicks away from finishing the pull request.

For more details, refer to http://docs.julialang.org/en/release-0.3/manual/packages/#publishing-your-package.

Graphics in Julia

Several packages exist to plot data and visualize data relations, which are as follows:

- `Winston`: (refer to the *Packages* section in *Chapter 1, Installing the Julia Platform*) This package offers 2D MATLAB-like plotting through an easy `plot(x, y)` command. Add a graphic to an existing plot with `oplot()`, and save it in the PNG, EPS, PDF, or SVG format with `savefig()`. From within a script, use `display(p1)`, where `p1` is the plot object to make the plot appear. For a complete code example, refer to `Chapter 10\winston.jl` (use it in the REPL). For more information, see the excellent docs at `http://winston.readthedocs.org/en/latest/` and `https://github.com/nolta/Winston.jl` for the package itself.

- `PyPlot`: (refer to the *Installing and working with IJulia* section in *Chapter 1, Installing the Julia Platform*) This package needs Python and matplotlib installed and works with no overhead through the `PyCall` package.

  Here is a summary of the main commands:

  - `plot(y)`, `plot(x,y)` plots y versus x using the default line style and color

  - `semilogx(x,y)`, `semilogy(x,y)` for log scale plots

  - `title("A title")`, `xlabel("x-axis")`, and `ylabel("foo")` to set labels

  - `legend(["curve 1", "curve 2"], "northwest")` to write a legend at the upper-left side of the graph

  - `grid()`, `axis( "equal")` adds grid lines, and uses equal x and y scaling

  - `title(L"the curve $e^\sqrt{x}$")` sets the title with LaTeX equation

  - `savefig( "fig.png")`, `savefig( "fig.eps")` saves as the PNG or EPS image

- `Gadfly`: This provides ggplot2-like plotting package using data-driven documents (d3) and is very useful for statistical graphs. It renders publication quality graphics to PNG, PostScript, PDF, and SVG, for the last mode interactivity such as panning, zooming, and toggling. Here are some plotting commands (refer to `Chapter 10\gadfly.jl`, and use it in the REPL):

```
draw(SVG("gadfly.svg",6inch,3inch), plot([x -> x^2],0, 25))
pl = plot([x -> cos(x)/x], 5, 25)
draw(PNG("gadfly.png", 300, 100), pl)
```

We'll examine a concrete example in the next section. For more information, refer to http://gadflyjl.org/.

Using Gadfly on data

Let's apply `Gadfly` to visualize the histogram we made in the *Using DataFrames* section of *Chapter 8, I/O, Networking, and Parallel Computing,* when examining the quality of wine samples:

```
# see code in Chapter 8\DataFrames.jl:
using Gadfly
p = plot(df_quality, x="qual", y="no",
         Geom.bar(),Guide.title("Class distributions (\"quality\")"))
draw(PNG(14cm,10cm),p)
```

This produces the following output:

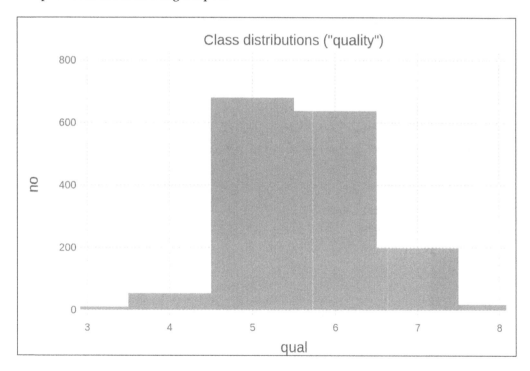

Here is an example to explore medical data: `medical.csv` is a file that contains the following columns: IX, Sex, Age, sBP, dBP, Drink, and BMI (IX is a number for each data line, sBP and dBP are systolic and diastolic blood pressure, Drink indicates whether the person drinks alcohol, and BMI is the body mass index).The following code reads in the data in a DataFrame df file that contains 50 lines and seven columns:

```
# code in Chapter 10\medical.jl
using Gadfly, DataFrames
df = readtable("medical.csv")
print("size is ", size(df)) #> size is (50,7)
df[1:3, 1:size(df,2)]
# data sample:
IX   Sex  Age  sBP     dBP   Drink  BMI
0    1    39   106.0   70.0  0      26.97
1    2    46   121.0   81.0  0      28.73
2    1    48   127.5   80.0  1      25.34
```

Let's transform our data a bit. The data for Sex contains 1 for female, 2 for male. Let's change that to F and M respectively. Similarly, change 0 to N and 1 to Y for the Drink data. DataFrames has a handy `ifelse` function ready for just this purpose:

```
# transforming the data:
df[:Sex] = ifelse(df[:Sex].==1, "F", "M")
df[:Drink] = ifelse(df[:Drink].==1, "Y", "N")
df[1:3, 1:size(df,2)]
# transformed data sample:
IX   Sex  Age  sBP     dBP   Drink  BMI
0    F    39   106.0   70.0  N      26.97
1    M    46   121.0   81.0  N      28.73
2    F    48   127.5   80.0  Y      25.34
```

Use `describe(df)` to get some statistical numbers on the data. For example, the standard deviation on the Age value is given by `std(df["Age"])` that gives 8.1941.

Let's plot systolic blood pressure versus age, using a different color for male and female, and apply data smoothing to draw a continuous line through the histogram rendered in a browser:

```
set_default_plot_size(20cm, 12cm)
plot(df, x="Age", y="sBP", color="Sex", Geom.smooth,
  Geom.bar(position=:dodge))
```

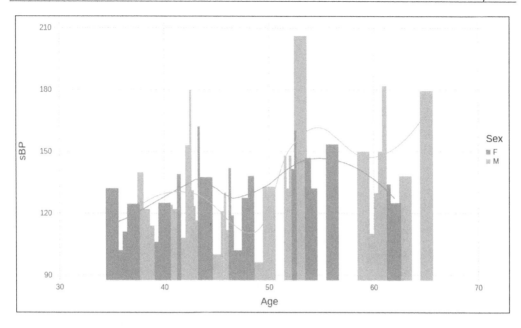

If you want to save the image in a file, give the plot a name and pass that name to the `draw` function:

```
pl = plot(df, x="Age", y="sBP", color="Sex", Geom.smooth, Geom.
bar(position=:dodge))
draw(PDF("medical.pdf", 6inch, 3inch), pl)
```

Lots of other plots can be drawn in Gadfly, such as scatter plots, 2D histograms, and box plots.

Summary

In this chapter, we looked at the built-in functionality Julia has to offer in its standard library. We also peeked at some of the more useful packages to apply in the data sciences.

We hope that this whirlwind overview of Julia has shown you why Julia is a rising star in the world of scientific computing and (big) data applications and that, you will take it up in your projects.

List of Macros and Packages

Macros

Chapter	Name	Section
2	@printf	The *Formatting numbers and strings* section under the *Strings* heading
	@sprintf	The *Formatting numbers and strings* section under the *Strings* heading
3	@which	*Generic functions and multiple dispatch*
	@time	*Generic functions and multiple dispatch*
	@elapsed	*Generic functions and multiple dispatch*
4	@task	*Tasks*
7	@assert	The *Testing* section under the *Built-in macros* heading
	@test	The *Testing* section under the *Built-in macros* heading
	@test_approx_eq	The *Testing* section under the *Built-in macros* heading
	@test_approx_eq_eps	The *Testing* section under the *Built-in macros* heading
	@show	The *Debugging* section under the *Built-in macros* heading
	@timed	The *Benchmarking* section under the *Built-in macros* heading
	@allocated	The *Benchmarking* section under the *Built-in macros* heading
	@async	The *Starting a task* section under the *Built-in macros* heading (also refer to *Chapter 8, I/O, Networking, and Parallel Computing*)

Chapter	Name	Section
8	@data	*Using DataFrames*
	@spawnat	Parallel Programming, *Using low-level communications*
	@async	*Working with TCP Sockets and servers*
	@sync	*Working with TCP Sockets and servers*
	@spawn	Parallel Programming, *Using low-level communications*
	@spawnat	Parallel Programming, *Using low-level communications*
	@everywhere	Parallel Programming, *Using low-level communications*
	@parallel	Parallel Programming, *Parallel loops and maps*
9	@windows	*Running External Programs*
	@unix	*Running External Programs*
	@linux	*Running External Programs*
	@osx	*Running External Programs*
	@inbounds	*Performance tips*
	@profile	*Performance tips*

List of packages

Chapter	Name	Section
The Rationale for Julia	MATLAB	*A comparison with other languages for the data scientist*
	Rif	*A comparison with other languages for the data scientist*
	PyCall	*A comparison with other languages for the data scientist*
1	Winston	*Packages*
	IJulia	*Installing and working with IJulia*
	PyPlot	*Installing and working with IJulia*
	ZMQ	*Installing Sublime-IJulia*
	Jewel	*Installing Juno*
2	Dates	*Dates and Times* (<= v 0.3)
	TimeZones	*Dates and Times* (>= v 0.4)
5	ImmutableArrays	*Matrices*
	Compat	*Dictionaries*

Chapter	Name	Section
8	DataFrames	*Using DataFrames*
	DataArrays	*Using DataFrames*
	RDatasets	*Using DataFrames*
	JSON	*Using DataFrames*
	LightXML	*Using DataFrames*
	YAML	*Using DataFrames*
	HDF5	*Using DataFrames*
	IniFile	*Using DataFrames*
	ODBC	ODBC
9	Cpp	*Calling C and FORTRAN*
	Clang	*Calling C and FORTRAN*
	Lint	*Performance tips*
	TypeCheck	*Performance tips*
	ProfileView	*Performance tips*
10	Gadfly	*Graphics in Julia*

Index

S

SageMath project
  URL 31
scope 54, 56, 82-84
sets
  about 100, 101
  of tuples, creating 101
shell commands
  running 169, 170
single dispatch 70
slice 50
splice operator (splat) 53
standard input (stdin) 139, 140
standard library 179-181
standard output (stdout) 139, 140
stream-oriented 139
string interpolation 170
strings
  about 43-45
  and formatting numbers 45, 46
  array of chars, converting to 53
Sublime-IJulia
  installing 30
  URL 30
Sublime Text
  URL 31
subtypes function 109
super function 108

T

tasks 84, 86, 136
TCP servers
  working with 152-154
TCP sockets
  working with 152-154
Transmission Control Protocol (TCP/IP) 152
tuples
  about 94, 95
  set, creating 101
type annotations 106
type conversions 107
type hierarchy
  about 108
  subtypes 109
  supertypes 108

type parameters 121, 122
types 38, 39
type unions 119, 120
typing 105

U

Ubuntu version, Julia
  Julia, building from source 19, 20
  OS X 19
user-defined type
  about 112
  multiple dispatch, example 115-117
  objects 114
  values 114

V

variables 36, 37
vector 88
Vim
  URL 31

W

while loops 77
Windows version, Julia
  about 16, 18
  URL 18
Winston
  about 184
  URL 184

Thank you for buying
Getting Started with Julia Programming

About Packt Publishing

Packt, pronounced 'packed', published its first book, *Mastering phpMyAdmin for Effective MySQL Management*, in April 2004, and subsequently continued to specialize in publishing highly focused books on specific technologies and solutions.

Our books and publications share the experiences of your fellow IT professionals in adapting and customizing today's systems, applications, and frameworks. Our solution-based books give you the knowledge and power to customize the software and technologies you're using to get the job done. Packt books are more specific and less general than the IT books you have seen in the past. Our unique business model allows us to bring you more focused information, giving you more of what you need to know, and less of what you don't.

Packt is a modern yet unique publishing company that focuses on producing quality, cutting-edge books for communities of developers, administrators, and newbies alike. For more information, please visit our website at www.packtpub.com.

About Packt Open Source

In 2010, Packt launched two new brands, Packt Open Source and Packt Enterprise, in order to continue its focus on specialization. This book is part of the Packt Open Source brand, home to books published on software built around open source licenses, and offering information to anybody from advanced developers to budding web designers. The Open Source brand also runs Packt's Open Source Royalty Scheme, by which Packt gives a royalty to each open source project about whose software a book is sold.

Writing for Packt

We welcome all inquiries from people who are interested in authoring. Book proposals should be sent to author@packtpub.com. If your book idea is still at an early stage and you would like to discuss it first before writing a formal book proposal, then please contact us; one of our commissioning editors will get in touch with you.

We're not just looking for published authors; if you have strong technical skills but no writing experience, our experienced editors can help you develop a writing career, or simply get some additional reward for your expertise.

open source*
community experience distilled

Practical Data Science Cookbook

ISBN: 978-1-78398-024-6   Paperback: 396 pages

89 hands-on recipes to help you complete real-world data science projects in R and Python

1. Learn about the data science pipeline and use it to acquire, clean, analyze, and visualize data.

2. Understand critical concepts in data science in the context of multiple projects.

3. Expand your numerical programming skills through step-by-step code examples and learn more about the robust features of R and Python.

Practical Data Analysis

ISBN: 978-1-78328-099-5   Paperback: 360 pages

Transform, model, and visualize your data through hands-on projects, developed in open source tools

1. Explore how to analyze your data in various innovative ways and turn them into insight.

2. Learn to use the D3.js visualization tool for exploratory data analysis.

3. Understand how to work with graphs and social data analysis.

Please check **www.PacktPub.com** for information on our titles

33001394R00119

Made in the USA
Middletown, DE
10 January 2019